MINISTERING CHILDREN:

A TALE

BY

MARIA LOUISA CHARLESWORTH,

AUTHOR OF "ENGLAND'S YEOMAN," "OLIVER OF THE MILL" AND "DOROTHY COPE

Complete in One Vol.

NEW YORK:
ROBERT CARTER & BROTHERS,
No. 530 BROADWAY.

MINISTERING CHILDREN:

VOL. II.

"And they say unto Him, Hearest Thou what these say? And Jesus saith unto them, Yea; have ye never read, Out of the mouth of babes and sucklings Thou hast perfected praise?"—Mat . xxi. 16.

CONTENTS

OF VOL. II.

MINISTERING CHILDREN.

I.

Learning to Knit.

"The words that I speak unto you, they are spirit, and they are life."—
John vi. 63.

WHILE Patience in the workhouse was gathering other children round her, and teaching them the blessed words that had so long lain silently in her own heart, little Jane, led by her mother's thoughtful care, had a ministry of love to the aged. In the town where Mr. Mansfield lived, there stood in a narrow street, a row of old almshouses; the walls were of white plaster; the one single shutter to each lower lattice-window, and the doors were black; and the old chimneys rose thick above the red tiled roof. In the spring of the year an old man and woman passed under the almshouse door-way, and up the white deal stairs, to end their days in one of the almshouse-rooms, which the friendly compassion of some people in the town had obtained for them. They had come from a large farm-house, where much had been under their care; but the old man had failed in business, and now all was gone—except one four-post bedstead with its white dimity hangings, their two arm-chairs, a chest of drawers a small round table before the fire, and a square one in the window, and such few other articles as were necessary to the furniture of one room. The old woman spread a white cover on the little table in the window, and hung at both small lattices muslin blinds, and to a stranger's eye the room looked a picture of neatness and comfort, and the old people were thankful for such a refuge; still they felt the difference, the old woman most of the two —and her stirring active manner changed to a look of silent dejection. They knew not that HOPE that can shed its brightness no less on poverty than on wealth, and is the only abiding light of either.

Mrs. Mansfield had known something of them in their better days, and now she hastened to visit them in their affliction; she saw their silent dejection, and the thought occurred to her mind, that very probably it was as much owing to the loss of all active interest in life as it was to any sense of present poverty; and that to provide the old woman a little employment might prove a great help in cheering their spirits. She knew also that Mrs. Blake was a good knitter; so after sitting with them in sympathy a short time, she said, "I have a little plan to propose to you, Mrs. Blake; I know you are a superior knitter, I want my eldest little girl to learn, and if you would not object to take a little pupil, I would send her to you three times a week for an hour, and then send for her again. I should willingly pay a shilling a week for her instruction, till she can manage it well enough to go on by herself."

"I am sure I should be thankful," replied Mrs. Blake, "it would seem a little company, and cheer us up every way!" So the next day was fixed for a beginning.

"Jane," said Mrs. Mansfield, that afternoon, "I am going to send you to-morrow to take your first lesson in knitting; you are going to a kind old woman who is willing to teach you. I am sure you will be very attentive, and try not to give her any trouble."

"Is she very old, mamma?"

"I dare say you would think her very old, so you must be careful not to tire her by making her tell you the same thing over a great many times. You know you have often wished you could knit like me, and now you will learn."

Jane took the first opportunity of getting off to the nursery, being always anxious to tell all that concerned herself to her nurse.

"Nurse, I am going to learn to knit like mamma; there is a very old woman who is going to teach me; mamma says I shall think her a VERY old woman! Do you think, nurse, I can do anything for her?"

"Yes, to be sure; I never saw the old woman yet that a child could not be a comfort to, if there was the mind to try!"

"What do you think I can do, nurse?"

"How should I know? that's for you to find out when you are there!"

Little Jane had no love for suspense, and she thought it would be much pleasanter to know at once just what she could do for this very old woman, and though it was her nurse who had taught her to reverence old age, still her mother was always her final appeal, so she did not stay long in the nursery, but made her way back again to her mother's side.

"Mamma, nurse says I can do something for the old woman. What can I do?"

"I hope you will be her little comforter, Jane, and that will be doing the best thing for her, for she is very sorrowful."

"How can I be her comforter, mamma?"

"Only by loving her, and trying to make her happy, as you try to make me when I am sad."

"I read to you out of the Bible to comfort you, mamma, will that comfort the old woman?"

"Yes, I hope it will. You will find an old man also, the old woman's husband, and when you have knitted three-quarters of an hour, you can tell them that you read to me to make me happy, and that if they will let you, you will read to them."

"How shall I know when it is three-quarters of an hour, mamma?"

"Mr. Blake, the old man, has a watch, and he will tell you if you ask him."

Now little Jane was perfectly satisfied, and with her path before her, clear and bright as the shining light, she waited for her next day's lesson.

Her nurse led her to the almshouse, up the white deal staircase, knocked at the black door where the No. 3 was painted in large white letters, and left Jane seated on a stool by Mrs. Blake's side. Jane was a timid child, and she felt a little strange when left alone with the old people; but she remembered that she was to try and be a comfort to them, and any sense of power soon dispels the slavery of fear. Jane tried to do her best, but the knitting-pins were strangers to her little fingers, and she longed to get to the pages of the Bible to which those same little fingers had long been used.

"Is it three-quarters of an hour yet, do you think?" asked Jane of Mrs. Blake.

"No, my dear, not more than one quarter as yet, I should say."

Jane knitted on in patience, but the time seemed very long, while she grasped as tight as possible the pins, which as yet she knew not the skill of holding with easier pressure. "Do you think it is nearly three-quarters now?" At length she asked again. Then the old man's pity awoke, and taking out his watch, he laid it on the table by the child, and said, "There, dear, now you can see for yourself!"

"I don't know what's o'clock when I look!" said little Jane.

"Come, wife," said Mr. Blake, "you have had time enough for your teachings; I will give mine now. Come here, dear, and I will shew you all about it!" So Jane stood at the old man's knee, and he taught her to find out what was o'clock, and spun out his lesson till the three-quarters were fairly over.

"Is it quite three-quarters?" asked Jane.

"Yes, dear; do you want to be going?"

"No, I don't want to go, but mamma said, would you like me to read in the Bible to you when it was three quarters of an hour?"

"Yes, to be sure!" said the old man. "Wife, where's our Bible?"

"It's here where it always is," said Mrs. Blake, going to the chest of drawers, "but it's too big for a child!"

"I can stand at the table," said little Jane, "I can find the place where I read to mamma this morning—I can find places in the Bible now all by myself!—shall I read what I read to mamma about the sheep and the goats?"

"Yes, dear, that's just what I should like!" said the old farmer.

M. C.

So the child stood up between the two old people, and her young voice bore on its feeble breath the seed of eternal life—herself unconscious of the enduring influence of the words that "are spirit and life," thinking only of its present power to comfort.

When Jane had done, the old man said, "Ah, dear, those are cutting words!" but Mrs. Blake only praised little Jane's reading. Jane looked at her, surprised and disappointed—she had expected a far higher result than any thought of her reading, and she said, gravely, "It makes mamma happy when I read her the Bible!"

"Ah, dear, that's as it should be!" said the old man.

"Does it make you happy?" asked little Jane, turning to him.

"God grant it may! God grant it may!" he replied, and little Jane, satisfied with his words, shut up the great Bible. Mrs. Blake saw that she had commented wrong, and that the child had expected what was read to have some effect on her; she said no more then, but she determined next time to listen, that she might see whether she could find anything in the words themselves. Then rising up, Mrs. Blake went to her closet and brought out her wheaten loaf and slice of butter, and cutting some bread and butter for Jane, she offered it to her. She had been used to bring out her home-made cake and wine to her guests; and now, though bread and butter was all her store, she would still offer that. Little Jane received the offer of the poor old woman as she would have received the same kind care from the rich; and then, her nurse arriving, she returned to her home, to give to her mother her simple account of all that had passed. And on through the summer weeks little Jane knitted her three quarters of an hour, then told the time from the old man's watch, and read her chapter out of the great Bible—And thus the child became a ministering guide to Heaven!

Before we leave the town we will pay a farewell visit to the shoemaker's family. We saw them before, on the Christmas-eve; and it was still the winter-time, when, if you could have looked in of an evening after the day's work was done, and when the mother's candle was lighted, and she was sitting by the round table at work, you would have seen on the table a pile of loose pages, and Agnes and Ephraim seated side by side, sorting and arranging them; they were pages of the New Testament, which Miss Wilson had found in one of the school-closets—a heap of old and torn copies of the Holy Testament; so she sent them to the shoemaker's bookbinding son, to see what he could do with them. He set his little brother and sister to work, and every evening, at their mother's side, they sorted the sacred pages, till they had some Testaments complete, and some separate Gospels complete, and some Epistles complete; then the bookbinding boy carried them off, and in his spare time, with the pieces his master allowed him to use, he put them all into neat dark covers, and then he gave them to Miss Wilson, saying, "I have not money, but I have a little time to give, and I want it to be my offering to those that have need!" He brought eight volumes—Testaments and parts of Testaments, refusing any payment, leaving the words that are "spirit and life," again ready for the use of the poor and needy. So it was that the shoemaker's children ministered to others "according to their ability."

While little Patience gathered health and strength in the warm summer-time beneath the workhouse matron's care, the life of the young sweet lady of the Hall was passing from the Earth. Every one around her watched her gently fading from their sight; her parents knew that she was dying, and looked upon her day by day—as if each look might be their last upon her living form; the servants watched her whenever in their sight, and thought of all that devoted service could do—as if they felt each act might be the last that loving reverence could offer her; the villagers looked from their labour when the carriage passed—and if she were in it, they turned and watched it out of sight; the cottage women looked from door or window, then sighing turned again to their work within; the very children of the village knew that their lady was departing, and looked into her face with silent questioning, which there was none to answer—for their young hearts spoke by looks alone; all knew that she had well-nigh reached Heaven's gate, all but her own young brother—he looked on her, but her smile, unchanged, still threw its veil of beaut yover weakness and pain, he looked no deeper than that smile, and thought that however her strength might change, that smile would be always beside him; and lest he should find that others thought differently, he never asked of any what they thought, and so he knew it not, but still believed that with the greatest care, she might recover again, as she had done before. It was now some weeks since he had been to old Willy's; for the last time he went, and expressed his hope that his sister would soon be well again, old Willy had shaken his head; Herbert saw and felt that shake of the old man's head; he said nothing, but he kept away from the cottage after that, afraid to venture again.

It was the close of June, the air breathed fragrance of the new-mown grass over the hills, the song of the birds was hushed at mid-day, and the heavy foliage hung its soft shade between the earth and sky. Miss Clifford came down in her shawl and bonnet, and Herbert, ever on the watch, soon had her leaning on his arm, crossing the unsheltered lawn. "You will not go this way, Mary, you will want the shade of the trees," he said—without arresting by a pause the frail steps he supported.

"No, I want to go this way to-day," she replied; "and as I cannot talk while walking, we will sit down on this seat, and I will tell you why."

Herbert sat down beside his sister, and she said, "There is a poor old woman who lives not far from the Lime-avenue Lodge, she is very ill, I fear they think her dying, and I want to go to-day and visit her."

Indeed, Mary, you must not go! you know mamma never lets you go and sit in sick rooms; and now, when you cannot take a little walk without being tired, I am sure you must not go!"

"Yes, dear Herbert, mamma does not mind to-day, she knows I am going, and you will go with me. I fear the poor woman is dying without a hope beyond the grave, and there is no one to tell her 'of the precious blood that cleanseth from all sin.'"

Herbert was silent; he thought,—could he go and tell the dying woman of the precious blood of Jesus, that could cleanse her from her sins? No, he thought he could not; he feared he should not know what to say to her; he had never seen sickness and death, and he was afraid to venture; so he let his sister take his arm, and he led her gently on: they were silent till they reached the cottage. The dying woman was lying on a bed put up for her in the lower room; she looked towards Miss Clifford, but did not speak. Herbert stayed by the open casement, and his sister went to the bed-side. "I am sorry to see you so ill," said Miss Clifford.

"O, dear, yes, and I am as bad in mind as I am in body!" the dying woman replied.

"What is it that troubles you?" Miss Clifford asked.

"What is it! why it's everything, even to the look of peace on my husband's face—for to my belief the peace he has is as much above my reach as the Heaven itself!"

"It is the peace of God your husband has, the peace of one who has found the Saviour; none ever reached that peace of themselves; but God, who gave it to him, can give it also to you."

"Yes, I know that I ought to repent; I know there is no mercy without that; but I don't feel it! so it's no use to say I do."

"You cannot get repentance any more than peace, of yourself, they are both the gift of God, but it is written in the Bible, 'Ask, and it shall be given you.'"

"Yes, I dare say it's all to be had by those

who have not set themselves against it all their life-long as I have done; but there's none can tell how I have turned against it—therefore there's none can say that it's for me!"

"Shall I tell you what God, who knows all things, says in His Word?"

"Yes, I don't mind hearing now!"

"He says, 'O Israel, thou hast destroyed thyself, but in Me is thy help found!'"

The dying woman looked up, those words, "Thou hast destroyed thyself," reached the depth of her sense of misery, they included it all, and made her feel that if over those "destroyed" there was hope, then might there be a hope for her! Clasping her hands together, and fixing her dying eyes upon the young speaker, she exclaimed, "Oh how you comfort me!" then, closing her eyes, she listened while again the same words, which had proved so instantly "spirit and life" to her, were repeated. After telling her of Jesus—mighty to save, on whom that help for the sinful has been laid, and whose precious blood can cleanse from all sin, Miss Clifford left the dying woman to the hope she had set before her in the Gospel. That one declaration of Divine truth, which, admitting all her sin and misery, turned her eye, not on herself for repentance, but on Jesus for help, had touched her heart; the seed of hope was planted, and in the last great day it may be seen to have brought forth fruit to life eternal.

Herbert led his sister gently home; he laid her on the couch to rest—wearied with her effort she did not speak, but putting her hand upon his head, she smiled upon him—one long sweet smile that met his anxious and inquiring look: then Herbert turned away thoughtfully to his room, he had a purpose in going there—it was to take his Bible in his hand, to hold again, himself, in his own hand the wondrous Book, whose words, from his sister's lips, he had but just seen change the face of restless dull despair to the earnest gaze of sudden hope. He held his Bible, he looked upon its pages, he saw the words so thickly traced, and thought again upon the living, the creative power he had but now seen them possessed of, and he resolved that the highest object of his life should be to make them his own by hiding them within his heart—that he might both live himself by their help, and use them in aid of others. He held the sacred volume as the young soldier grasps his sword—for personal and relative defence; but Herbert's was "the sword of the Spirit, the word of God"—which wounds but to heal; which destroys—not man, but sin, man's enemy; a sword given to be used—not to defend one human being against another, but to defend all against the powers of evil, to rescue all from Satan's dreadful dominion. Happy the child who goes forth early in this blessed warfare—who, taking the Word of God, first proves its power in his own heart and life, then tries to use it for the good of others; he "shall stand in the evil day, and having done all, shall stand;" and those beside him, whom God will give him to be his glory and jóy in the day of Christ's appearing.

II.

"She is Gone!"

"O, I stand trembling
Where foot of mortal ne'er hath been;
Wrapped in the radiance of that sinless land
Which eye hath never seen.

"Bright visions come and go;
Shapes of resplendent beauty round me throng;
From angel-lips I seem to hear the flow
Of soft and holy song."

It was the summer night. The cloudless heavens were gleaming with their host of countless stars; the village slept in the calm hush of midnight's hour, it slept and knew not that its best and dearest treasure was passing from its sight for ever. Horse-hoofs trod swiftly through the village street, but they roused not the labourer whose healthful sleep is sweet to him after the long day's toil; then all was silent, till after an hour's space, carriage-wheels rolled rapidly by; it sounded like the doctor's carriage, and affection's wakeful ear and heart were roused, many a villager listened, some looked anxiously out; but the distant sound had died away, and all was silent again. With the dawn the village rose. "Man goeth forth to his work and to his labour till the evening." Far over the bright pastures, the grass had withered, the flower faded, beneath the mower's scythe; and one, the sweetest flower that ever grew within the village bound, one that every village hand would have been raised to shield and to retain, had fallen too beneath the scythe of Death—the young sweet lady of the Hall lay dead; that night her spirit had departed, and the place that had known her knew her no more. The villagers soon learned the tidings, and one told another, till every cottage knew and mourned its loss. Yet they said not, "She is DEAD;" but only, "She is GONE!" They thought not of death, but of Heaven as her portion; so they said one to another, "She is gone!" and the labourer raised his arm, from turning the new-made hay, and wiped away the tear that dimmed his eye; and the widow wept alone within her cottage-door; and the village mother, silent and sad, prepared the morning meal; and the children cried beside their untasted food—the village mourned; for the friend, the loved of all was gone!

The windows of the Hall were curtained—and silence dwelt around it; guarding the still repose of that lovely form in death, which it had sheltered through life. The grief of the home was calmed by the near approach to Heaven's gate with the bright spirit who had, manifestly to all, entered in; and for a time the glory that received her struggled with the sadness her departure had left behind—even as the sun's parting rays cast their light back on the grey shades of advancing twilight. Poor Herbert alone had been surprised as by a sudden shock, he knew not that she was going, till, lo, she was gone! Grief held him in its heavy fetters, he could think of and feel nothing but the first overpowering sense of death and desolation; he knew too little yet of what it is to rise in heart and live in Heaven, to be able to feel communion of spirit still, with her whom he had lost from Earth.

The day of the funeral came, and the whole village gathered to the grave—there came the old and feeble, whom her hands had clothed and fed, her lips had taught and comforted; there came the dark transgressor whose chains of sin had melted under her fervent utterance of Heavenly truth and love; there came the strong-built labourer, whose dull mind had gathered light under her gentle teaching, whose hand of iron strength had followed her frail finger, tracing out the sacred lesson of holy writ; there came the village children, the lambs of the Chief Shepherd's fold, whom she had fed with the living Word of the Lord of Life — all came to see the form they had loved laid to its rest, till the resurrection of the just. Respect brought some but it was love unfeigned that led the many there; they filled the churchyard, lined the wooded lane that led down the hill-side, reached to the park-gate and stood beneath the trees that grew beside it. Old Willy had climbed the hill, and leaning on his staff, stood beneath the churchyard Yew. Then the long procession came in sight, the servants of her home would suffer no hired hand to bear her honoured form, and lay it to its rest; slowly they came, the snow-white border of the sable pall gleaming between the old trees of the park;—telling of purity and light that encompasseth the blessed, hidden from earthly sight by the dark shade of death. Herbert was led by his father, and the long train of mourners followed. There stood the mourning village, and the mourners from many a village round. The great men of the Earth have a name through its generations, and then—if their greatness has been of Earth only, their very name must pass away and be lost for ever; but the childlike spirit, who lives to minister to other's good, to ease the burden of the weary-hearted, to sweeten and bless life's bitter cup, to win the lost to the Saviour's feet; luring on, by words of truth, and bright example of Heavenly Love, from Earth to Heaven, from darkness into light, from death to life; has a record written on human hearts—hearts whose records are eternal! A suppressed sob heaved the breasts of the villagers as she—who had ever come among them in life to bless—was borne into the midst of them sleeping in death. The village children had filled their pinafores with the summer flowers, they had been wont to gather them to win her smile, and now they cast them down before the feet of those who bore her to her rest;—she who most endeared the flowers to them had passed away from Earth for ever!

The clergyman of the village, an old man, had served that village-church for thirty years; but not a single voice had blessed him, for he knew not the power of that love by which the minister of Christ unlocks the sinner's heart. He had now stepped from his garden to the vestry on the other side of the church, and it was not till called to meet the departed, that he saw the assembled village. As the sight from the church-porch first broke upon him, he stood for a moment overcome, such a company of mourning people—children whose sobs answered to the silent tears of strong-built men and helpless age, was grief too real not to raise the instant question within him, "What woke this burst of love?" and he stood silent and awestruck at the church's porch. Meanwhile the bearers waited; they had reached the churchyard gate, and would not enter without the words of holiest greeting for the beloved form they bore! then, in that moment's solemn pause, old Willy,

OLD WILLY IN THE CHURCHYARD.

standing beneath the Yew, raised his voice, and calmly and distinctly exclaimed, "Welcome, the holy dead!" At the sound of those firm tones of age, the Minister recovered speech; he came forward with the words of Life, and the bearers followed him into the church. The service went calmly on; but when the white coffin was borne within the tomb, overcome by the hopelessness with which they hid his sister from his sight for ever upon Earth, Herbert fainted and fell. The servants came forward, but meanwhile Jem had darted through them, and kneeling on one knee at Herbert's side, looked up at the father's face for permission to raise the boy; the servants would have put him aside, but the father moved his hand to them to retire, and lifting Herbert from the ground, placed him in the arms of the faithful Jem, sending a servant hastily forward to prevent needless alarm to Mrs. Clifford. The throng separated for Jem to pass, bearing his precious burden—the child of fortune, the only hope of his father's house, trusted to one of themselves, borne by the village lad to his home. Jem made his way down the hill-side, then stopped a moment to raise the boy's arm which had fallen from its posture of rest, and as he laid the small soft hand on the breast of the boy, he thought of the day when he had taught it first to use the tools sc large and heavy for its strength, in labour for the poor and needy! and the tear of past and present feeling gathered in the eyes of the faithful Jem. Jem was met on his way to the Hall, and accompanied by some of the maid-servants to the house. Mrs. Clifford waited anxiously within the door.

"It's only a fainting, ma'am," said Jem, "it was all over too much for my young master, but he will come to, quick enough now!"

Mrs. Clifford bent a moment over the fainting boy, almost as pale herself—her vision almost as dim. "Bring him in here and lay him down," she said; and she opened the nearest door, while the maids gathered to the hall, bearing various remedies and helps. Mrs. Clifford preceded Jem into the dining-room—the very room where Jem had stood alone with the young Squire to receive his mother's scarlet cloak.

"Come in and lay him here," said Mrs. Clifford, and she placed the damask cushion for the boy's unconscious head. Jem had felt no hesitation in raising the heir of that stately mansion in his arms to bear him to his home; but now that by daylight he saw the rich carpet that lay before his feet, he held back with his precious burden, hesitating in his rough shoes to tread upon a thing so costly! even so it is that the poorest can rise in a moment to feel and act upon the universal tie of nature's one brotherhood, but they pause at the threshold of wealth's display; and own, as if by instinct, that the separating line lies there!

"Bring him in," repeated the housekeeper; and friends within the house were gathering, and maid-servants were waiting round, and so Jem bore the child of the mansion across the rich carpeted floor, laid him gently down with his pale cheek on the crimson cushion, and then as he stepped back, while Herbert's mother knelt beside the couch, and friends drew near and servants waited, Jem bowing, asked, "Will you please that I should fetch the doctor?" but the housekeeper shook her head and whispered, "No;" then Jem, with another bow of the lowliest reverence, and a look of anxious love towards the fainting boy, withdrew. He saw the long train of mourners descending the hill, and made his way straight to the farm, there to solace himself among his sheep.

The evening shadows fell and closed that summer day; the folded flowers, the folded flocks, the birds with folded wing—all sought repose; while softly calm the moon rose over all in the blue heavens. Old Willy had vainly tried to comfort his troubled heart—his eyes were dim, so that he could not see the words of the Book! he sat awhile within doors, then stepped into his garden, then back again within the cottage in wearied restlessness, wanting some human voice to fall on his aching heart with tones of comfort! but all that summer day were mourners, and no earthly com forter drew near. When the hush of evening shed its soothing silence round, and sleep seemed far away from old Willy's tear-dimmed eyes, he took his staff, and set forth to climb once more that day the steep hill-side; and look upon the tomb where they had laid his blessed guide to Heaven. All were gone from the hill-side; and the Hall, with its far-stretching slopes, lay silent and beautiful in the summer evening twilight. Old Willy looked round once from the hill-top on his lady's home on Earth, then turned to the churchyard gate, and leaning upon it, rested there a little while before he ventured further, for the place where they had laid her seemed to the old man holy ground—too sacred almost for his feet to enter. So he leaned upon the gate, looking on into the distant azure of the sky, looking almost without sight or thought, his senses lost in one deep feeling—they had laid his blessed teacher in the grave, they had left her there alone, the night was darkening over her, and he alone kept watch above the form so loved of all! How long he stood he did not know; but suddenly he saw in those blue heavens before his eyes a shining star; full on his sight its radiance beamed; the only star in heaven, risen there in view, and looking down to comfort *him*, it seemed! "Ah! sure I see it," the old man said in a low tone; "sure, I see it's no use looking down in the dark grave for her that's up above the stars in glory there! I see it!" again he murmured low, as with a lingering gaze on that bright star he turned to depart; but then again he looked towards the tomb, and thought he would stand beside it once before the night came on; and so he climbed the stile beside the now-locked gate, and reached the silent grave; then stopping short, gazed in surprise, for at its foot a child lay sleeping, her head reclined against the lady's tomb, her lap full of fresh-gathered flowers. "Poor dear!" said the old man, "she has fallen off asleep; why, 'tis little Mercy Jones! Mercy, child! I say, wake up there!" And the child sprang up from sleep like a startled fawn, and her flowers dropped from her pinafore; but when she saw it was old Willy, she stood still, looking down on the fallen flowers.

"Why, Mercy, child, you must not stay sleeping here, it's no place for you!"

"Yes, but it is," said the child, without looking up, "it's the best place in all the world—to be near to my lady! I have not been so near to her since that last day she came and stood among us all in school; she smiled at me then! but I can't see her now. Oh, if I could but see her!" And the child sat down again at the tomb's foot, beside her fallen flowers, and hid her face and wept.

The tears again dimmed old Willy's eyes; but

still he saw that beauteous star shining so brightly down from the blue heaven—looking full upon both him and the young child, as they watched there beside the tomb within the churchyard dreary, and he answered quickly, "Why, child, your blessed lady is not here! look there, she's shining bright in Heaven!" The child looked up with sudden start, as if expecting that angel face to beam upon her from above, or to get some distant glimpse of her lady's white-robed form in glory; she looked where the old man pointed, and her eye too rested on the star—on those calm blue heavens above her, and that beaming star so full of softened glory—she looked, then said, "I only see a star!"

"Well, child, what more would you see? Is not that star enough? isn't it just come, shining down from heaven, to tell you that the blessed lady is up above it far away in glory? For what did God send it in the sky, if not to put you in mind that there's a world of glory up above, all shining bright like that same star, and that He took the blessed lady straight up to it to dwell with Him for ever?"

"Yes, I know it," said little Mercy, "and I wish I was with her there!"

"Then, child, you must be walking the path she went!"

"What path was that?" asked Mercy, looking up to the old man's face.

"Why, the blessed path of love, child! love to God and man; her mind was always on her Saviour, and trying to bring others to the love of Him. Oh, child! it's written in the Book that "GOD IS LOVE," and there's none but a path of love that can lead up to Him!"

Little Mercy was silent; she had tried to tread the path of love, in which her lady had taught her to walk, she had tried to please God her Heavenly Father, and Jesus her Saviour, and to be a ministering child to others; and now she knew not what more to do; all looked dull and dreary around her, and she was silent.

"Come now, child," then old Willy said, "it's best to begin at once! You know right well your poor grandmother is fretting at home for that blessed lady that's gone; now, do you go back, and be cheerful, and comfort her up!"

"Yes," said little Mercy, "I came here because I could not bear it,—Granny cried, and said, 'the summer-time seemed gone from the Earth!' and though I had set the supper all ready, uncle Jem turned away and never eat a bit! so I went and gathered those flowers and came here."

"Well, child, you know you have seen that star; there it is, look at it, see how it shines right down upon us here—a bit of glory as it is! Now, you go and be like that, you go and try! He who sent that star to light us up with comfort here, sent you to your good grandmother to be a bit of light to her in this lonesome world—you mind that, and go and try, till the day comes when you will go, as the blessed lady's gone, to Heaven!"

So little Mercy rose, and took her bonnet from the ground, and the old man laid his hand upon her head, and blessed her, and she left her fallen flowers at the foot of the tomb, and back she went with many a look upon the star in the blue sky; from whatever point she turned to look, the star still beamed upon her,—seemed to watch her still; so she went back with light in her eyes and fresh life in her young heart, gathered from the old man's words, and the bright star in Heaven. Old Willy, too, went home, and from his cottage-door beheld the same bright star; then laid him down to rest—to sleep and dream of glory.

III.

Snowflake.

"The memory of the just is blessed."—Prov. x. 7.
"Being dead, yet speaketh."—Heb. xi. 4.

THE old clergyman could not forget the scene he had witnessed, but the love and the sorrow were both incomprehensible to him; he felt their reality, but could not understand their cause. At length it occurred to him, how often, in driving out, he had seen Miss Clifford's ponies at the cottage-doors; he concluded that it must be the notice she had taken of the Poor that had endeared her to them; and thinking it would be pleasant to win the same feeling for himself; pleasant to have the love of all his people in life, and their tears above his grave, he determined to visit, himself, from house to house with this object. He thought also that it would be pleasant to be kind to those who showed so much feeling, such warm return of gratitude! so he set forth. He went through the village street, calling at every house, leaving his gift of money, and saying a few words to all, but he returned dissatisfied;

he had met no smile of welcome, seen no tear dimmed eye grow bright; heard no blessing. What made the difference? Why had he no power, and she—the departed, so young in years! why had she so much? He could not tell; he did not know that a difference, as real as that of Earth and Heaven, lay between his visits, and the visits of her the village mourned. He had gone in his own name, his words were of Earth, his gifts the dole of the richer to the poorer; his object was to please, and to win affection and gratitude to himself; but she they mourned had gone to none but in the name of JESUS; her words breathed to all the love and truth of Heaven; her gifts were ever the expression of her thoughtful sympathy—warm with compassion's tenderness, and bright with the glad power of ministering aid; such was her way of giving, that her gift ever elevated, instead of seeming to degrade or lower the receiver; her highest object was, not to win feeling towards herself, but to win the whole heart and life of those she visited to her Saviour and their Saviour, that they might be happy in Him, and He glorified in them; therefore an overflowing recompense was poured out for her—for "with what measure ye mete, it shall be measured to you again." But the aged clergyman knew not that the difference between his Earthly kindness, and her Heavenly love, was wide as the east is from the west. He was disappointed, and resolved to give up the vain attempt, and go on as before. But then a recollection of that old man who had stood within the churchyard gate, and uttered those words of blessing on the departed crossed his mind, and he resolved to go and call on him, and see what he would say.

Old Willy saw his minister coming up his cottage-garden, and stood at his door to receive him: old Willy had learned to behave himself lowly and reverently to those whom God had placed above him in station, and courteously to all. There is no such teacher of true courtesy as pure Religion—if we would only learn of her!

"Sit down, my good friend, sit down," said the clergyman. "What a nice house you have here! I think I remember this quite a tumble-down building?"

"Very like you may, sir; for that was the fashion of it many a long day!"

"I think I saw you at Miss Clifford's funeral the other day?" observed the clergyman.

Old Willy sobbed out, "Yes, sir!" overcome at the sudden mention of the subject.

"Never mind, my good friend, I am sorry to distress you! I suppose Miss Clifford was very good to the poor?"

"Ah, yes, sir! if I might have given my old life for hers, there's hundreds would have blessed me!"

"Miss Clifford came to see you, I suppose?"

"Yes, sir, sure enough she did, but it was Him she brought with her that made her wholly a blessing!"

"Who was that?" asked the minister.

"Why our Saviour, sir! she never went anywhere to my belief without Him, and you never saw her but you seemed to get a fresh sight of Him."

The clergyman was silent; at length he said, "Well, my good friend, you come very regular to church, I wish I could see a few more of your neighbours there."

"Yes, sir, but then you see we want teaching! and there's some of them that can walk after that."

"To be sure they want teaching! and have not I preached two sermons every Sunday for thirty years? Why don't they come to hear them?"

"That's true enough, sir, there's none can say to the contrary of that; no doubt there's teaching enough in your sermons to do anybody good; only poor dark creatures as we are, can't get hold of it because the Light isn't set up in the midst of it!"

"What light do you mean?"

"Why, sir, I mean Him that is the Light of the world, without whom 'tis groping in the dark—I mean our Saviour, sir! why, when one gets a sight of Him, then one can see and get a hold of all the good that lies round; but when there's no getting a sight of Him, why, it seems all the same as leading a poor creature out when the sun is not in the sky—there's no getting a right understanding of anything!"

The aged minister was silent again; old Willy waited, but when the silence lasted, he laid his hand upon the Bible at his side, saying, "I never look in here for teaching, but I see Him before me! He is just the very light of my old heart, that was as dark as death before. I first got a sight of Him out of this Book, and now I never so much as look into it but I see Him, and I find it holds but dark where there's no setting up of Him!"

"Well, my good friend, I will think of your words," said the old clergyman, and so saying withdrew.

The summer sun had three times risen and set since Herbert sank beside his sister's grave: he was lying on his mother's couch, his cheek almost as pale as then; his Bible lay beside him, he had ceased to read, and on his face rested a look of sad and earnest thought; his mother watched him anxiously, but feared to question him, lest she should but wake her own deep grief and his into expression.

"Mamma," at last he said, "you see it is harder for me than for any one!"

"What is harder?" asked Mrs. Clifford.

"To lose Mary, mamma."

"Why is it harder for you, dear Herbert?"

"Because you and papa are so good! but I was always getting wrong, and never should have got right again if it had not been for Mary's smile."

Mrs. Clifford was silent, she could not question more on such a subject. Herbert soon went on to say,

"You see, mamma, when I got into trouble, you and papa of course were displeased; and you looked so grave, and then I lost all hope in a moment, and it was so dreadful to feel as if one could never be right again! And I never felt as if I could, or seemed to know how; but when I went to Mary, she always smiled at me still, and said she knew I was sorry, and wanted to be right again—and so I am sure I did, though I did not always know it till she told me; and then she used to say it would soon be all bright again; and when I looked at her, and heard her say so, I believed it, and then I tried, and she used to tell me what to do, and help me; and then I was sure to get right again; only you and papa did not know how! But now I don't see any hope for me, I don't know what will become of me!"

"Do you know who gave you your sweet sister to help you on your way?"

"Yes, mamma, of course it was God."

"And has God, your Heavenly Father, given you no better gift—one that still remains, one that death can never take away?"

"Yes, mamma, I know that God has given us Jesus Christ, and that He helps me when I pray to Him; I know that, mamma; but then I cannot see Him, or hear Him speak to me, as I could Mary!"

"You have not seen Him yet perhaps, dear Herbert, but you may see Him! He can and He does show Himself as clearly to the eye of the spirits of His children sometimes, as earthly objects are seen by the eye of the body; and He speaks as distinctly to their hearts as earthly voices to the ear."

"But would Jesus smile on me, mamma, when I get wrong, and am in trouble for it, as Mary used to do?"

"O, yes, He would! whatever may have been your fault, if you only turn to Him you will find His tenderness the same; His love, my child, is more than a mother's; and what His tenderness leads you to hope, His power can enable you to accomplish—He can work in you both to will and to do according to His own good pleasure."

Herbert lay silent, thinking on his mother's words; and she had gathered strength from speaking of Him who is the Life, to speak of her whom death had taken; and went on to say to her listening child, "It was so with Mary; she lived always in the presence of God her Saviour, and in the sense of His love; it was her greatest joy to try in all she did to please Him, by doing His holy will—this made her life so happy and so blessed!"

Then Herbert said, "I will try, mamma, and do as Mary did! Shall I read you a chapter from the Bible now?"

"Yes, dear Herbert, that will help us both to do that of which we have been speaking—even to walk in the light of God's countenance." So Herbert read to his mother; and the words of Heavenly Truth and Love lightened the sadness of their hearts, as the rising sun illumines the mist that hides the heavens from our earthly view.

Days passed away, and Herbert returned to his studies; but the paleness did not pass from his cheeks, nor the sadness from his brow; he had not mounted Araby, nor taken a single walk by himself since the day that saw him bereft of his sister. He was sitting one morning in the window of his father's study with a lesson-book before him; but his eyes were far away on the park's green slopes, where the deer were feeding. His father came in, and, going up to him, laid his hand upon the boy's dark clustering curls; but silently, as if he feared to wake into expression the saddened thought so plainly written on his face. Her bert looked up; then, after a minute's silence, said, "Papa, shall I tell you of what I was thinking?"

"Yes, my boy, what was it?"

"I was thinking that I wished Snowflake might be unshod and turned into the Park, to live always there, and no one ever ride her again; she would look so beautiful under the green trees! I am sure she has done good enough to rest all her life now, and I could not bear to see her led up for any one else to mount."

"No, perhaps none of us could bear that; but how would it be if I had a new pony-carriage for your mamma, and you drove Snowflake and the groom's pony in it? and then we could keep David on, and have a seat behind the little carriage for him, to save your mother's fears?"

"O yes, papa, I should like that! I had not been into the stables till to-day, and David took the cloth off Snowflake, she looked as beautiful as possible, and turned her bright eye round on me, only she looked so sad; I am sure she knows, papa: any one who saw her would think so too! David said that at first he felt as if he could not bear the place, but now he feels as if he could do anything to stay. May I tell him what you mean to do, papa? I know he will be so glad!"

"Yes, if your mother does not object. Jenks can try Snowflake alone in the pony-chair. I know he broke her in first to that."

"Yes, papa, and then I can drive mamma out first with Snowflake alone, till the new carriage comes!" And Herbert rose up with more of purpose and energy than he had felt since the day that the stroke of bereavement had first fallen on him. Mrs. Clifford made no objection; any personal fear being overcome by the sense of the new interest for her child. David met the proposal still to stay as groom very gratefully; and Jenks said, "You could not put the creature to the thing she would not do if she had the power!" So it was finally settled, that after one or two days' trial by Jenks, Herbert should drive his mother with Snowflake in the pony-chair, till the new carriage could be bought.

The day arrived when Herbert was, for the first time, to drive his mother out. Old Jenks led up the pony-chair with Snowflake harnessed in it; she did not stand with arching neck and pawing step, but sorrowfully with head hung down; as if she knew that the hand and voice she loved would not be now awaiting her. Herbert felt all the responsibility of his new privilege; and some unexpressed anxiety that all should be prosperous in this his first attempt to drive his mother, helped to check his feeling at sight of Snowflake. Mrs. Clifford also was not free from nervous apprehensions, never really considering herself safe except when old Jenks was her charioteer—she had only yielded to the proposal for the sake of the interest to Herbert; and now her feeling also at sight of the snow-white creature was lessened by a sense of personal apprehension; she took her seat, and Herbert his, by her side, and Snowflake gently trotted from the door. There were only three roads by which to leave the Hall for a drive; one was the direct way to the town, and led past old Willy's cottage; Herbert had not yet summoned courage to see old Willy, though the old man had been many times up to the Hall to inquire for him, since the day he had seen "the blessed child," as he called him, fall beside the grave; therefore Herbert would not go that way, because of passing his cottage. Another road led up the steep hill-side to the church, past the churchyard gate, and then round by farmer Smith's, a longer way to the town; that could not be ventured on; so Herbert drove out by the gamekeeper's lodge, and took a long winding shady lane that led round by the back of the park. Snowflake trotted swiftly and smoothly along; but gentle as the creature was known to be, Mrs. Clifford was still on the watch for fear of some mischance. On they went beneath the sheltering trees, when, drawing near a lonely cottage, Snowflake suddenly quickened her pace and drew up at the door.

"What is the matter!" exclaimed Mrs. Clifford. Herbert touched Snowflake with the whip; but all the advance gained was a few steps to a little window of one pane, rather high up in the wall—a window that opened with a push from within or without, directly underneath which Snowflake took a determined stand. Herbert gave her a harder stroke; she shook her silver mane at the unwonted indignity, but did not move a step. Herbert's colour mounted to his cheeks, and Mrs. Clifford exclaimed, "Take care, Herbert, something will certainly happen!" At that instant the door opened, and out came a neatly-dressed woman, curtseying, as if to expected guests.

"Do go to the creature's head while we get out!" said Mrs. Clifford. The woman obeyed, and Herbert sprang down and handed out his mother.

"Something is wrong!" said Mrs. Clifford, as she stood on the door-step, "the creature will not move!"

"O dear me, no, ma'am, the pretty dear is always used to stop here; I don't know I have ever seen it pass by without!"

"What for?" asked Mrs. Clifford.

"Why, you see, ma'am, my poor old mother is blind and bed-ridden, and that sweet lady that's gone was the very light of her life, and I never saw her so much as pass by once! She used to get off at this door-step, and the pretty creature knew it as well, and would never have wanted the telling; and if she was all in a hurry for time, as she would be sometimes, why then she just rode up to that little window—it goes open with a shove, and it's just above my old mother's bed, and there she would speak a cheery word to her and then be off again; and, dear me, how that word would lift up my poor mother's spirits! She used to say, the very sound of her voice was like Heaven's music to her, sent to comfort her up in her darkness! So that is all the meaning of the pretty creature's holding to it so!"

The sudden alarm Mrs. Clifford had taken, and now the sudden disclosure of the cause, were too much for her; she stepped into the cottage, and sitting down, leaned her face upon her hand, and wept. Herbert threw his arms round Snowflake, partly to hide his tears, and partly to atone for the stroke of the whip he had made her feel. The poor woman waited beside Mrs. Clifford in distress to know what to do, then hasted and brought her water in a glass. Mrs. Clifford soon recovered self-possession, and turning to the poor woman, said, "I will see your mother." The woman hastened into the inner room, and smoothing the bed-clothes, whispered, "Here's Madam herself from the Hall! the pretty creature would not stir a step, and Madam is wholly overcome!" Then, hastening back again, she took Mrs. Clifford in. Mrs. Clifford went to the bed, took the old woman's hand in hers, and sat down, but vain were all attempts to speak; the poor old woman felt her silent grief, but while the big tears from her sightless eyes rolled down her cheeks, she said, "Oh! my lady, this world is the place for weeping, but the blessed dear has gone to Him who wipes all tears away! Don't I see her with my sightless eyes, shining as bright as the morning's ray up above in the holy Heaven? and don't it lighten me up, as the sound of her tongue did here! I never thought to hear her horse's feet ring down the lane again; and now that you should come! 'tis a wonderful condescension and lifts me up—that it does!"

"I will come and see you often!" replied Mrs. Clifford, and she rose, strengthened by the old woman's vision of faith, but unable to say more, pressed her hand, and left the cottage.

It was the first visit Mrs. Clifford had ever paid to the poor and needy. The deep feeling and touching expression, the unassuming attention, the bright faith beholding what her own faith had not realized—all these surprised her with their charm; that brief visit had planted in her heart the seeds of a personal interest in the poor; she felt too the peace of having shed comfort on another, and she stepped from the cottage-door, unwilling so soon to leave the spot, yet feeling unable then to stay. The fear too of safety with Snowflake seemed lost in the deeper impressions now awakened, and a creature who could so follow the track of its departed mistress's steps of love was surely worthy of confidence; so Mrs. Clifford took her seat by Herbert's side, and ceased to look out for occasions of mischance.

On through the summer lanes they drove, and the sweet air relieved the oppression of feeling. The drive was a lonely one, farm-houses and cottages among the fields, but none by the road-side, till at the foot of a hill, sideways from the winding lane, stood a cottage; a little boy was standing beside the wicket-gate, clad in a coarse round pinafore, his little cap crushed up in his hand, left his fair curls uncovered, and his smiling eyes of blue looked down the winding lane as if with listening expectation.

The boy was Rose's little friend, Johnnie Lambert, the widow Lambert's only child. Quick as thought, the listening boy at sight of Snowflake darted into the cottage, calling "Mother! the lady's coming!" then back he ran to the wicket-gate, while the mother looked from the door.

"Stop and let us speak to that child," said Mrs. Clifford, for she saw the white pony was well known to the boy.

The child made his deliberate and never-forgotten bow, then raised his bright face as if to meet the look of some loved familiar friend; but instantly the blank of disappointed hope chased his glad smile away, and running to the pony's head, he sheltered himself there.

Seeing the pony stopping at the gate, the mother stepped out and curtsied low.

"Your little boy knows the pony?" said Mrs. Clifford.

"Yes, ma'am,—Johnnie, come here and make your bow to the lady!" but Johnnie was giving his tears to Snowflake. "He takes on, ma'am, so about the dear young lady that's better off, he is always watching for her, and I can't make him sensible that she is gone! he ran in just now, for he thought it was her when he got sight of the pony."

"Was she often here?" asked Mrs. Clifford.

"O yes, that she was! All the time my poor husband kept about, she used to come and read to him—for he could not read a word, and I never saw a man so changed! he suffered a wonderful deal, for his complaint lay in the head; and nothing could ease it, and he lost all his spirits, and was always fretting to live and get well; but when she had showed him the way to Heaven—all plain for him to walk in, and showed him how his Saviour called him to come unto Him! he seemed to think of nothing else, it was wholly a pleasure instead of a misery to see him!"

"Has he been long dead?" asked Mrs. Clifford.

"Over two years, ma'am; but to me it seems

all as fresh as yesterday! He lay six weeks in his bed; and all that time he never saw the dear young lady, only she used to send and inquire for him; but he seemed past the want of her then, though before when he was about he would sit all day long and watch for her coming by; but when he took to his bed, and she could not come, he seemed to be hanging only on his Saviour. I have heard him say when I sat by his bed, 'Oh, I see Him! I see Him!' and then he would let me leave him and get my night's rest—though he could not sleep a wink for pain, but it seemed as if Heaven had opened above him. Oh, it was a wonderful change! he said the dear young lady's words had been life from the dead to him!"

Herbert had slipped out of the carriage unperceived by his mother, and now standing with the reins in his hand, was trying to comfort the child; but he could not get him to speak, only to take a shy look at him now and then.

"Poor dear!" said the mother, looking round, "it puts me so in mind of his father to see how he listens for the creature's feet;—the dear young lady took wonderful notice of him! he can say many a thing she taught him, only he's shy. When I ask him where his poor father is, he will point up to the sky, and say, 'With God!' but I can't make him sensible that the dear young lady won't be coming down the lane again!"

"Tell him that we will come again!" said Mrs. Clifford—with an effort to retain composure; and Herbert hearing this assurance, took his seat, and they drove on—watched out of sight by the widow and her orphan boy.

But now it was necessary to decide which way to return—either back through the lanes, and so risk another halt at the blind widow's door; or past the churchyard gate! or by old Willy's cottage. Herbert preferred the last—as best of the three, and before they reached the old man's dwelling, they saw him in the distance, advancing slowly on the road towards them.

"There is old Willy himself!" said Herbert.

"Do not pass him by," replied Mrs. Clifford, "stop and speak to him."

The old man stood some minutes beside the little carriage, his white head uncovered--the very picture of beautiful old age! Mrs. Clifford talked to him, and with true refinement the old man made no reference to the one of whom each heart was full, his feeling only struggled through in silent tears; he had changed away his week-day garment for an old coat of black, and in this, and a band of crape about his hat, wore the signs of mourning for her who had been more than child to him. At parting, Mrs. Clifford said, "I shall come and see you with my son."

"A thousand thanks!" replied old Willy, as he

bowed low to the lady, but his look of love turned full and rested on Herbert.

"Yes, I shall soon come, Willy, very soon, and mamma too!" added Herbert, greatly relieved at the thought of the first sight of his aged friend being over.

And so they returned to the Hall; both had passed through much to try them in that morning drive, but not less to soothe and elevate. The mother and the son felt as if they had that day entered on their sweet Mary's path of love and service, and they longed to follow her steps in all. Herbert now often drove his mother out; all fear of Snowflake was gone; the creature was allowed to stop at pleasure; and when a visit could not be made, some kindly word was spoken, till in every dwelling where her child had shed the light of hope, and the peace of comfort, or the aid of knowledge, Mrs. Clifford followed her; gathering the blessed recompense that even the most aching heart must find in keeping God's commandments —watered herself with heavenly consolation in watering others. While in Herbert's young heart —so trained and disciplined, Earth daily gathered more of Heaven; and a depth of feeling and a power of thought and action beyond his years, enriched his life with personal and relative happiness.

IV.

Patience at Service.

"Bear ye one another's burdens, and so fulfil the law of Christ."—Galatians, vi. 2.

THE summer months left Patience in the workhouse restored to health. And now another place of service must be found for her; the workhouse made the choice, and we shall find what it was. Patience took leave of her workhouse home with a sorrowful heart; and a heavy dread came over her as she drew near the place to which she was now engaged. It was a small house, a short distance out of the town; and from the number of children crowded together in one room, it might have been taken for an infant-school! But no, it was a family of ten children; the youngest a baby of some few weeks, the next just able to step alone, the third a helpless little cripple, the fourth a rosy-faced girl of about five years of age,—then twin-boys of seven, with the four elder boys and girls, went to a day-school.

This was now to be the place of service Patience was to fill; maid of all work in the family of the foreman in Mr. Mansfield's shop; ten children, and all the washing done at home! It sounds like heavy work, but we must not, like old nurse Brame, be led by sound alone; and we may always remember that work proving hard or pleasant depends far more upon the minds of those who rule and those who serve, than upon the amount of labour to be done. Patience arriving at the house, knocked at the door a low timid knock. Robert, the eldest boy, opened the door, and then ran back to his mother to say the new girl was there. "Bring her in then," said the mother; so in came Patience, still pale and fearful, with her small bundle in her hand. "Come in, come in and see us all at once!" said the mother and mistress, without so much as making a moment's stop in her washing. Then, looking hard at Patience in the fire-light, she added, "What's that all the show you have to make of strength! Well, if you are killed with hard work, that will lie at your master's door, for it was he hired you, not I, remember that! Here's plenty of work—and plenty of play too, so don't be frightened! There, Betsy, you go and show the girl where to put her bonnet and shawl and her bundle, and then don't lose a minute, but come and be after tea." Betsy did as she was desired, and quickly returned with Patience to the kitchen. The autumn evening was damp and cold, and when

Patience returned to the family party, preparations for tea were beginning. The little parlour opened into the small kitchen, and Robert, the eldest boy, was kneeling down before the parlour-stove, blowing up the flame he had just lighted. Polly, the second girl, was setting out the tea-things; and the moment Betsy returned, she began to take her part in fetching out the bread and butter and cheese, together with a large round cake, whose only claim to the designation consisted in a few scattered currants—more thought of because so far apart that each one became a definite object, and this so-called plum-cake, with its scanty sweetening of sugar, was much more approved by the little group of children than slices of bread and butter. Patience had not been five minutes in the house, but on no account was she to stand idle. "What's your name, child?" inquired the mother, still ringing out the wet clothes, and depositing them, one by one, in a large white basket. "Patience!" replied the new little servant.

"Patience! Well, I have heard worse names than that! You may be sure you will have plenty of need of patience here, though there is no hardship for all that! I hope you have an apron?"

"Yes, in my bundle," replied Patience.

"Have it on then, as fast as you can!" And up stairs ran Patience with a light, quick step; there was something so animating in the universal stir below stairs, that she longed to be one among them all again, and in two minutes time she stood aproned before her mistress.

"Now take that wide shovel and gather up all those cinders by the grate here, and put them every one on the parlour fire." So Patience gathered up the cinders, and laid them on the top of the nobs of coal, among which the cheerful blaze began to ascend. "Now take the kettle and fill it at the tap there, and set it on this fire to boil," said her mistress. Meanwhile Robert had been out and shut the shutter; Betsy had drawn the chintz curtain within; Polly had lighted one solitary candle and set it in the middle of the tea-table; the mother had wrung out the last little garment—and the whole collection lay piled in the large white basket; the water was poured from the washing-tub, the tub set up, the stool on which it stood put aside, the whole kitchen then looked in perfect order, the mother drew down her sleeves, changed her coarse blue apron for a white one, and in they went all to tea. The baby sleeping in its cradle had woke up some minutes before; but Betsy had lifted it out and rocked it in her arms, till the mother, seated in the low black chair beside the parlour-fire, received it. The children dragged out their stools and chairs; little Esther, the child of five years—not having yet learned the division of labour, pulled hard at a parlour-chair for herself with one hand, and at the poor little cripple's high chair with the other. Patience caught sight, amidst the active group, of little Esther's attempt, and, running up to her, reached over her head, and laying hold of both chairs, pulled gently also, when, to the child's perfect satisfaction, both chairs moved slowly and steadily to the table. Esther would by no means leave her hold till the chairs were drawn quite close, so Patience slipped behind them and pushed, till the little Esther, stooping half under the table, peeped up with a grave look, and suffered Patience to lift her into the parlour-chair, gravely observing, "I did pull two chairs!" And through the heart of Patience passed a warm feeling for the child; and a sense of active life, with its native charm of cheerful energy, rose still more freshly within her at this first successful aid rendered to the child. And now Betsy placed the little cripple in his chair, and Esther looked up at Betsy, repeating, "I did pull two chairs!" and Betsy said, "Good Esther!" and hastened away to fix up the next baby of eighteen months old. Now there was one small blue plate set down between Esther and the little cripple; Esther put her hand upon it by way of claim, but did not take it nearer, then the little cripple reached out his hand and said, "Me! me!" Esther shook her head—for it was hard to give up the plate that was the earnest to her of food; but Patience, whose attention was all alive, caught sight of the difficulty, and put another blue plate close before Esther, who then pushed the other gently to her little brother, and, looking up at Patience, said, "I did give it him!"

All the little ones being seated, Betsy cut the bread and butter, Robert a piece of cake for each, Polly filled the mugs half full of water, and poured water into the tea-pot for the tea, while all the little ones looked on. This divided labour was quickly accomplished, after which the mother stood up with the babe in her arms, the elder children stood also, and Robert asked the blessing —for at meals, when the father was away, this was always Robert's office. Patience had a corner at the table, and made as hearty a meal as any of them: the good mother seeing her hesitate at first, took care to say, "Come, Patience, girl, make haste, you have earned your tea, though you may not think it!" There was no riot at the meal; the children, trained in good order, found no pleasure in confusion; and having had no food since their early frugal dinner, their best amusement was to eat. All the play had come before tea, and now the moment it was over, and Robert had given thanks while every little one was silent with clasped hands, Betsy and Polly took off the baby of eighteen months and the little cripple each in their arms to bed, and the mother bid Patience follow with Esther, who looked very grave, but quite willing to go with her helper of the tea-table. Patience found that Esther was to share her little bed, in a room just large enough to hold the bed and one chair. The little cripple and the baby of eighteen months were soon laid to their sleep, and Betsy went down with Polly to bring up the twin boys of seven. When Patience returned to the parlour, the tea-table was cleared of all that had been used, and what remained was set in order for the father's return; the boys having so arranged the table, were already at their tasks for school the next day, and the mother putting the infant to rest. Patience was set to wash up the tea-things in the back-kitchen; while Betsy and Polly sat down to their lessons.

The baby slept in the cradle; and when Patience had finished washing up the tea-things, and had been shown where to put them away, her good mistress said, "now for your thimble as quick as possible!" And Patience had a seat at the table, and one of the children's socks given her to darn. But Patience was no darner, she had never been taught, for there are but few schools in which any trouble is taken to teach children to mend; though to the children of the poor the skill to mend well is hardly less needful than to make. Poor Patience felt her spirits sink; she could not do the work, and now she thought her troubles would begin, and the timid child, only so lately warmed with the glow of kindness, dreaded a sharp word more than anything. But sharp words were not given in this her new abode without a needs-be. The good mistress saw the colour rise to the pale face of Patience over the sock; so calling her to her, she said, "I can see you are no match for your task; well, never mind, bring your stool here, and sit down and learn, there will be no time lost in the end by good learning in the beginning!" So Patience took her seat by her mistress, and learned to darn, as little Jane had learned by her mother's side, only that Patience, being much older, learned to darn a great deal quicker, and did not want so much attention as Jane had done. While Patience darned, the four children who were sitting round the table repeated their lessons to their mother. They had had tea at five o'clock, and all their lessons were learned and repeated by eight, except those of the youngest boy. The moment the clock struck eight, the books were all put away, and the boy whose lessons were not learned, with a sorrowful face wished his mother "Good night," and went up to bed in the dark. This was done without a word being said, for it was the constant rule of the house; if the school lessons were not learned from six tc eight, no more time was given, as the lessons were not hard or long, and were learned in less time whenever the children were diligent; and the mother's principle was, neither in work nor lessons to allow time to be wasted. Then the girls sat down to their work of mending or making, and Robert to knitting—the boys never being idle when the girls were busy. Presently home came the father to their glad welcome; he sat down to his tea and supper both in one, while the mother and the children worked and talked, and Patience darned her sock.

As soon as the father's supper was over, Patience cleared all the things into the back-kitchen as directed; the great Bible was put on the table, the children brought theirs, Patience was sent to fetch hers—her own little Bible that Miss Wilson had taken her in her first place of service; and then father and mother and children all read a chapter, verse by verse, and Patience had to read with them; then the father questioned the children, and he questioned Patience also, and looked pleased with her answers; and then they all knelt down, and the father offered up the evening prayer. After this, Robert and the girls went to bed. Patience washed-up and put away the things from her master's supper; and then to her surprise she found her work was done; in fact everybody's work was done, for all the house was in order, and Patience went up to her closet of a room where little Esther lay sleeping. With what a thankful heart did the orphan child offer up her evening thanksgiving and prayer! and then taking her treasured half-crown — which she had kept through all her troubles and changes, she looked at it, and wished that beautiful Lady could but see how happy she was now! And she lay down to sleep—as if suddenly brought in the midst of a home's bright circle all her own!

The next morning her mistress called her at six o'clock, and to her mistress's surprise Patience came out from her closet ready dressed. She had heard her mistress rising, and risen herself.

"What, up and dressed!" said her mistress; "well, you mind my word, I never knew a bad servant an early riser! Now then, we shall be at work before the girls to-day!" And the pleasant stir soon began below. Patience had, as quick as time itself, to light up the back-kitchen fire; then to brighten up and lay the parlour-fire, while Betsy followed to sweep the room and dust the chairs; and while the chairs were dusting, Polly set the breakfast. Robert was out in the little garden fixing the linen poles; and Thomas, the second boy, chopping wood and filling the coal-scuttle, while the good mother fried bacon for the father's breakfast, and made the coffee. All as busy as possible, and all done by seven o'clock when the father came down; he had been reading his Bible in the midst of his six sleeping children, and now he came down to breakfast with his four eldest. Patience also was called to the table, and so they sat down to the morning meal. Each child repeated a text from the Holy Bible, and the father asked Patience if she could remember one, and Patience repeated the words—"I love them that love Me; and those that seek me early shall find Me." After breakfast, the father read a Psalm, then offered up the morning prayer, and hastened away to be at the shop by eight o'clock. Patience went up stairs with Betsy and Polly to dress the children—the mother prepared their breakfast; Robert worked in the little garden, which had its Autumn as well as its Spring and Summer flowers; but Thomas had to sit within and get his lessons perfect. At a quarter to nine, boys and girls were off to school; the twin-boys were taken to an infant-school by their elder brothers on their way to their own school: the poor little cripple played hour after hour on his sofa-bed with a doll; Esther talked to Patience and stepped about at her side, while the baby of eighteen months old sometimes played on the floor and sometimes slept. At twelve o'clock the children all came home, when, to the surprise of Patience, the baby of eighteen months and the little cripple were put into a light wooden carriage, and all the children went out for a walk together—Robert and Betsy taking the charge. Patience and her mistress ironed away till one o'clock, when they all returned. Betsy and Polly made ready the little ones; Robert and Thomas set the dinner-table, and all were seated with hungry appetite to eat the food provided for them.

Day after day passed on, till Patience felt more like an elder child and sister than a servant in the house. Betsy and Polly confided to her their secret hopes; Betsy's desire was to learn mantua-making, and be a lady's maid—as her mother had been before her; and to this end her mother trained her. Polly meant to be kitchen-maid first, and then cook, with the hope of being one day a housekeeper, and taking charge of stores—which seemed to her the most interesting of work; accordingly every jar and bottle in the house was put under Polly's keeping; she gave out the daily supply, wrote the labels, tied down the jars, made some preserves in the summer time, and took every opportunity of doing the cooking. Robert had a hope of being taken into Mr. Mansfield's shop, where his father was foreman; while Thomas had as yet no definite desire or prospect in life. Months passed away in this happy family, till all the paleness was gone from the cheek of Patience, and her figure, becoming strong and stout, seemed made for untiring work. She had taught Esther her own short morning and evening prayers—

learned by her when at school, and the little girl now never lay down at night or rose in the morning without offering them up. Her master was a subscriber to the Church Missionary Society; the children would often earn or save some offering for it also; and when Patience received her monthly wages, she always paid her sixpence to the same blessed object. A year passed away, and Patience went to call on Miss Wilson, but Miss Wilson did not know her—till on talking with her she found this rosy, strong, active-looking girl full of life and cheerful spirits, was the pale, thin, silent child, she had known so long at school! Patience told Miss Wilson of her happy life in her mistress's house—with ten children; herself maid-of-all-work, with all the washing done at home; and how the little one who slept with her, had learned her prayer and said it night and morning, and how her master subscribed to the Church Missionary Society—and she subscribed also. And there, in the midst of life and cheerfulness, we leave Patience for the present; and return to the village farm.

Rose had done with school, happy at the thought of living always at home. It was not long however before her happiness met her first sorrow in the loss of Miss Clifford—she had stood between her father and William at the funeral, and in the long summer days she and little Mercy had cried together. Then the yellow harvest came; and when the reaper's work was done, and the last sheaf carried, and William had stood aloft on the point of the high round stack with the last sheaf in his hand, before he laid it under his feet, and the men in a circle round him sung the "Harvest Home;" and the fields were left bare; and the thresher's flail sounded from the barn; then another sorrow came for little Rose—a sorrow for her home and for the farm; William had a good situation offered to him in a London shop. Farmer Smith's brother was a London linen-draper; William had always been a favourite with his uncle, and now his uncle's son had left the shop to follow a business he liked better, and the place of trust which he had held was offered to William, and a high salary was offered with it—for his uncle wished much to have him, and knowing William's love for the farm-work, he was afraid unless he made the offer very tempting, that it would be declined. But it was not money that would have tempted William away from his father's farm, if it had not been for the sake of his young brothers. It was some years since farmer Smith had been able to lay by any profits: in one bad farming year he had been obliged to borrow money on some cottages built by his mother, and left to him by her; he had been unable to pay the money or the interest upon it, and now the cottages were no longer his—they had become the property of the man who lent him the money—they had cleared him from debt, but he had nothing now beyond the yearly produce of his farm; and one bad farming year might put him in difficulty again. William worked like a labourer on the farm, and was worth two other men, because his mind and his heart were in all he did; but there were four younger boys, and farmer Smith knew not how he should provide for them. If William went to London, it was not unlikely that he might find situations for some of his brothers there. So farmer Smith decided that William should go—with a heavy heart he decided that William should go. William felt as if all the outward joy of life would be darkened for him—away from his home and his father's farm, shut up all day where fields were out of reach; but he chose the higher pleasure of doing that which would be most likely to relieve his father and aid his younger brothers. The boys thought it was a fine thing for William, to go to London! Rose tried to be as cheerful as she could, but Mrs. Smith never gave so much as one pleasant look, from the time it was decided for William to go.

Mr. Clifford was sitting alone in his study, when an impatient knock at his door roused him from his book. "Come in!" he said, in a tone that seemed to guess the intruder. Herbert entered, out of breath with haste.

"Papa, what do you think I have just heard in the village?—young Smith is going off directly to a situation in London, to a shop,—only think, papa! I would not lose such a fellow as he is from the place for anything, and I am sure he would not go if he could help it! don't you think something could be done to prevent it, papa?"

"We must first know whether his friends and himself would wish anything to be done to hinder his going; perhaps they may feel it to be to his future advantage to go, however sorry they may all be at present to lose him."

"Well then, papa, suppose I just go down to the farm and hear?"

"I think it would be wise to go and learn a little more what the facts of the case are, before you and I decide here what is to be done to prevent it!"

"Well, then, papa, so I will, and I will come back and tell you!"

And the father suffered the boy to go, unchecked in his warm impulse, to the farm. Seated in the farm-kitchen, he gave full expression to his thoughts and feelings on the subject: Mrs. Smith, for the first time, heard opposition to the plan equal to her own; she brought the young Squire her home-made wine and cake, but he was too intent on his subject to partake of such hospitality. Farmer Smith talked the subject long over with him, and, child as he was, told him the hopes he built on his eldest son's departure, as if he had been a long-trusted friend—a due recompense for the boy's warm feeling! Herbert returned to his father more than ever interested for the Smiths, and for William in particular—but convinced that it would not be the thing to attempt to hinder the London plan. Deep in William's heart sank the memory of the young Squire's unwillingness to lose him from the place—the warm feeling that had been expressed soothed the pain he felt at going; it cheered his father's heart to think how his son was valued by those above him; and even Mrs. Smith seemed more softened into gentleness on the subject, now she knew that her favourite William was not likely to be forgotten in his native village. Such the large results that oftentimes might follow—lasting on enduringly—from the spontaneous feeling and unchecked expression of childhood's true appreciation! When the autumn winds strewed the sere leaves upon the garden-paths at the farm, there was no neat and careful William to sweep them away—the great and busy city had received him.

Herbert's tutor did not find in his pupil the love of books that he naturally desired in one whom he had undertaken to prepare for study at college, and he communicated to Mr. Clifford his anxiety and regret, that Herbert, engaged by so many objects of interest, did not make the progress he could wish in his lessons.

Mr. Clifford replied, "It is very natural and very right, that you should feel anxious on such a subject; but we shall gain nothing by straining a point; no compulsion will implant the love of books; and we have need to remember that books are but prepared means for erecting the mental structure. A mere man of books is rather a ready made collection of materials, than a living influence. It is my belief that a circle of human life, gathered by sympathy's natural tie around a child, exercising every good and self-denying feeling the young spirit has, is likely to rear and leave a nobler character, far more excelling in power and influence, than the mere student of books. But I would not have you discouraged even as to Herbert's book-learning. I find him an increasingly intelligent companion, awake to every subject I bring before him, his mind free and unburdened by the weight of mere acquirement. He is following on in the right order—things Heavenly before things Earthly—the heart before the head; and though I may not live to see it, I am not without the hope that he, who as a child has learned to minister with such self-devotion to age and poverty, may yet bring down his country's blessing on his head!" The tutor pressed his patron's hand and withdrew.

V.

Darkness and Light.

"SON, REMEMBER!"—Luke, xvi. 25.

WHEN the next summer-time had come, filling the land with beauty, and fragrance, and plenty—telling of His rich bounty who "is kind to the unthankful and to the evil," "and sendeth rain on the just and the unjust," a messenger arrived at the Hall, asking to speak with Mr. Herbert Clifford.

"I am come from Mr. Sturgeon, sir," said the man, "he is very ill—thought to be dying, and he begs you to pay him a visit as soon as possible."

Herbert went to his father. When Mr. Clifford heard the request, he said, "Go, by all means." Herbert sent word by the messenger that he would follow immediately, and was soon on his way to Mr. Sturgeon's residence. Solemn thoughts filled his mind, he was sent for by a dying man—what could it be that Mr. Sturgeon wanted to see him for? Perhaps he wished before he died to do something for old Willy; but old Willy had all he wanted now!

Herbert arrived at the house, and one of Mr. Sturgeon's sons took him up at once to his father's room. The dying man looked at him, and said, "I thank you, sir, for coming so soon! You are the only person in all the world I wished to see; for you, dear young sir, are the only one who ever came to me with the words of faithful warning. I don't mean to blame my fellow-men; I have heard the best of preachers and the best of discourses, but from all these I could—I did shield myself. Oh, why did none come to me with the pointed arrow of truth, and say to me personally —'you are casting away eternal life!—you are putting Earth before Heaven!' You did come to me; you did warn me; and I wish to thank you for what might have been of eternal use to me if I had listened to your counsel."

Then Herbert took, not as before the smooth stone for his sling, but the balm of healing and life, from the Epistle of St. James—all of which he had learned by heart. "It is written in the Bible," said Herbert, "'The prayer of faith shall save the sick, and the Lord shall raise him up; and if he have committed sins they shall be forgiven him!'"

Mr. Sturgeon seemed not to hear, or not to heed the words of peace. "Oh, it is not the future, but the past," he went on to say, "that presses on my soul with its iron yoke—wherever

I turn I seem to hear a voice, and it says to me, "SON, REMEMBER!"—it says no more, but in those words there seems destruction. I do nothing but REMEMBER; and in remembrance there seems despair!"

"But," said Herbert, "our Saviour said we were to remember HIM—and that must be HOPE!"

"Yes, I know it—He said we were to remember HIM! and if I had remembered Him then, now I might have hope; but I have lived to forget Him—I have forgotten Him in the very church, where I professed to worship Him—I have forgotten Him in secret, where I might have found Him and made Him my own for ever—I have forgotten Him in business, where I have taken the customs of man, and not the heart-searching law of Christ for my rule—I have forgotten Him in the world, where I have been more careful to honour myself than to show forth His praise—I have forgotten Him in my so-called charities, for I still dared to give in my own name that which but for the gain of oppression, might never have been mine. Yes, I have forgotten Him; and now He knows me not!"

The dying man made no mention of old Willy; he could take a just estimate of sin now; and the sin of forgetting God, of thinking more of himself than of Him—the Lord of Glory—who died to open Heaven's gate to sinners, swallowed up the sense

OLD WILLY'S COTTAGE.

of all beside. He had sinned against old Willy; sinned against man, it was true; but the thought of this for a time was lost in the overpowering sense that he had sinned against Heaven and before God. The dying man gave Herbert his hand, and said, "Dear young sir! I can say no more; I wished to give you my thanks, and to tell you freely that you were right and I was wrong; and that 'the way of transgressors is hard!' May you reap the fruit of that truth which you tried in vain to plant in my heart!"

Herbert rode slowly and mournfully away.

The road home lay past old Willy's cottage; and there, in that warm summer afternoon, sat the old man on the bench beside his door, his hands resting on his staff, his broad-brimmed hat shading his eyes, and his head bowed in slumber; beside him bloomed the rose and honeysuckle, while over him hung the large leaves of the vine; Herbert's hand had planted them—meet emblems of the Earthly and the Heavenly love by which the old man's life was blessed! Herbert left his horse with the groom, and walked up the straight path to the cottage. Swiftly had he run up that same path at the head of the gamekeeper's boys, to rear up a blazing fire on old Willy's hearth: he had rushed up the same narrow path to shout the glad tidings to old Willy that the home of all his life was to be his dwelling still; he had hastened with light foot, bearing the old man's coat, his father's Christmas gift; but now his step was slower, for it bore to old Willy's side a heart oppressed with thought and feeling. Herbert felt as if he wanted to see the old man, to hear him tell of Heaven and his own bright hope, to dispel the gloom that had gathered round his spirit. Herbert went to old Willy, not now to give, but to receive. He stopped a little distance from the bench, unwilling to wake his aged friend; he stopped and looked at him; his feeble wasted frame, his white locks on his shoulders, his labour-worn hands; and that green life and fragrant blossoming of nature round him—its bright freshness in strong contrast with his withering form. Herbert felt how he loved that lone and frail old man; and as he felt how he loved him, he looked on the cottage his love had prepared; there rose the firm white walls, its close-fitting window and door, its warm and sheltering roof; there lay the little garden before it, where plant, and herb, and tree seemed to grow rejoicingly out of the ground—pleasant to the eye, and good for the food of that old man: and then in the hush of that summer afternoon, a still small voice spoke within Herbert's heart, and said, "Inasmuch as ye have done it unto one of the least of these my brethren, ye have done it unto Me!" Herbert looked up to the cloudless sky above his head, as if he thought to see Him whose words then spoke within him; he looked up, and he felt that old Willy's God and Saviour—and his God and Saviour—looked down in love on him; and the gloom and the weight were gone from his heart, and the light and the love of Heaven were there. Old Willy had slept in his young master's moment of need; but the God of all such as old Willy never slumbereth nor sleepeth, and He hath said "If thou draw out thy soul to the hungry, and satisfy the afflicted soul, then shall thy light rise in obscurity, and thy darkness as the noon-day!"

Now Herbert felt as if he no longer needed to stay and speak to old Willy, for heavenly peace had come without; and though he still felt solemnized and sad—for the sorrow he had witnessed of one who had lightly esteemed the Rock of our salvation, yet the chill and the gloom were gone, and his need supplied. But as he turned to go, old Willy raised his head, and seeing the young Squire turning away, he rose as quickly as he could, and taking off his hat, said "I beg your pardon, sir!"

"What for?" asked Herbert, as he turned again, and sitting down on the bench, laid his hand on old Willy's arm, making him sit down by his side.

"Do you know, Willy, that Mr. Sturgeon is dying?"

"No, sir; sure! not dying?"

"Yes, they think him dying! and he sent for me, to tell me that I was right when I pleaded for you; but oh, Willy, it was dreadful, for he has no hope, and I could not comfort him!"

"Well, master, 'tis better so, than if he had a false hope!"

"But nothing can be worse than NO HOPE, Willy, and he has NO HOPE!"

"Yes, master, 'tis better to feel it—If the true Hope be not there, 'tis better to have lost hold of every other; for then may-be they will feel after the true Hope and find it: may-be they will look up to their Saviour from the very gate of death itself, as the dying thief did; Oh what a look he cast upon the Lord!—And that look found salvation in the Saviour for him, and he went into Paradise with the Son of God!"

"Then, Willy, you think Mr. Sturgeon may find hope in our Saviour even now?"

"I pray God he may!" replied old Willy, fervently.

"Oh I wish he might!" exclaimed Herbert. And then giving a smile to old Willy, in which love and hope struggled with his lingering sadness of expression, he departed.

The dying man passed away from earth, and never could the boy, through life, forget the death-bed where the Saviour was not.

The traces of bereavement and sorrow began to be visibly marked in Mr. Clifford. The mother and the son had felt their loss no less, but a light had sprung up for them on every side, in the general service of love to which they had turned—they had taken their departed Mary's bright ministry, and the hearts that mourned for her, now looked to them for comfort. To Mrs. Clifford the personal work was new, and its results charmed her with the sweet surprise of a power to bless, comparatively untried before. And then she was not companionless in the work, her boy — her precious boy, once so wild and wilful, was her ardent companion, and shared the new interest to the full! But the father had lost the one, who, from life's earliest childhood, had walked and rode beside him, visited, studied, read with him; he found but one thing able to soothe the aching void her absence left—that one thing the Word of God! that was his solace now, it took his lost one's place. And it soon became evident how high the fountain of eternal Truth rises above its purest stream; how deep the well-spring of eternal Love, compared with the most purified of earthly vessels. Continual converse with the Divine Word irradiated all his life with Heavenly Light—the "conversation in Heaven," the constant thought for others, the tone of deeper feeling, the calmer firmness even of censure, all bore witness of a drawing nearer to the Home of perfect Love and Truth, a rising now in spirit to breathe more of its pure atmosphere while still on Earth. But failing health denied him all active effort; and his bowed form and feeble step told of Earth's decay. Change of scene and climate were urged as the only hope of imparting new vigour. Mr. Clifford at first refused but at last yielded to Mrs. Clifford's anxiety a reluctant consent; and arrangements were made without delay for going that Autumn to Italy.

When Mr. Clifford had consented to leave his home for a foreign land, he sent for the aged Minister of the Parish, and receiving him alone in his study, addressed him, saying, "I have sent for you, dear sir, to say to you as a dying man—which I believe myself to be; what I ought long ago to have said to you in health. You were appointed to hold the Lantern of the Word of Life to this people, but you show them not its Light; you preach its moral precepts, but that Saviour in whose light alone any can see the Light of Life, you show them not; and therefore all your teaching is dark and dead—unable to quicken one soul unto eternal Life, unable to guide one wanderer into the narrow way. I beseech you to consider what I say for your own sake, and the sake of your people. And let me entreat you to pray earnestly that the Spirit of Christ—by whom alone He can be revealed, may yet be given you to enlighten the eyes of your understanding, that you may yet know the sinner's only true ground of confidence—'Christ in you the hope of glory.' Forgive me for speaking plainly; alas! I ought years ago to have warned you in faithfulness, as I do now. I have also a request to make. I make it as the request of your dying patron—that you will allow me before I go, to provide a curate to aid you in your ministry here. I will furnish you with his yearly salary. I will promise that he shall be one who will walk in all lowliness towards you and towards all men,—one whom you may make a stay and comfort in your declining years; but one also who will teach and preach Jesus Christ—that Saviour who bore my dying child through the valley of the shadow of death, causing the dark valley for her to glow with the glory of His presence—that Saviour, to whom I look in humble hope of His infinite mercy to bear and carry me—that Saviour, dear sir, whom you will need; without whom there is no salvation—and it will be my earnest prayer that in hearing Him preached, you may be enabled 'to lay hold on the hope set before you.'"

The aged Minister did not refuse his Patron's wish, did not refuse to hearken unto counsel: it sounded to him as a thrice-repeated warning—first heard in the sobs of his people who wept at their young teacher's grave; then in old Willy's simple words; and now from the lips of one who had always treated him with kindness and consideration.

Before Mr. Clifford left, he assembled all his tenants and dependants to a dinner provided in his park. After the repast, the different groups were gathered in one, and Mr. Clifford came among them, his hand upon the shoulder of his boy, on whom he leaned; then uncovering his head, he said, in a voice distinctly heard, "My friends, I am going a long journey, and I wished to take my leave of you. I am not going by my own desire, for I would myself have chosen to abide the will of God here, whatever that will may be; but our own feelings must sometimes yield to the judgment of others. I wished before I left to thank you for the affection you have manifested towards me and mine. In the earlier days of my residence among you, some pain might have been spared to you and to me, if you had better understood my aims and wishes, and if I perhaps had had more skill and patience in making them known to you. But we have now, I believe, lived long enough in connection to gain mutual confidence. If there be any among you who have any grievance, past or present, to complain of, I ask them, with all friendliness of feeling, towards them, to come and state it to me before I go, that, God permitting, I may leave no thorn behind in any heart without the prayerful effort to remove it thence. For all in which I have been wanting towards you, I ask your forgiveness in the sight of Heaven; and most of all, that I have not done more to teach you the good and the right way. I have desired you should know it, but I have made too little effort to accomplish that desire. I pray you, seek it for yourselves more earnestly than I have sought it for you; for the promise that they shall find the Lord and Giver of Life, is given to none but those who seek Him with all their heart. One blessed child I had who lived and died among you, and I may safely say to you, 'Be ye followers of her, as she was of Christ!' I commend my son to your prayers, that he may have grace from above to commend himself to your affections. And now, my friends, 'I commend you to God, and to the Word of His grace, which is able to build you up, and to give you an inheritance among all them which are sanctified, through faith which is in Christ Jesus.'"

Thus it was the Squire took his leave. One thing more he did; and that was to have a white marble slab raised on the wall within the village church, where all the poor could see it; and on it was written his daughter's name, and age, and place of residence; and this text, "Remember ye not, that when I was with you, I told you these things?"

Herbert took leave of old Willy. "Never mind, dear Willy!" said the boy, with choking utterance, "I shall come back again to take care of you; I shall never forget you, and you will live here in quiet, and everybody will be kind to you when they know I am gone!" And the old man blessed him, weeping! The family drove from the Hall—the road-side lined with those who mourned their loss: they left their home for a foreign land. There, with the same devotion with which he had watched his dying sister, Herbert tended his dying parent; and the natural impetuosity of his character deepened into quiet strength. Mr. Clifford lived six months abroad, and then he died. He said, "I have not the same radiant sunbeam of faith that lighted my Mary's steps through the valley of the shadow of death; but I have the peace of an assured hope that my Saviour hath loved me, and washed me from my sins in His own blood; and that because He lives, I shall live also!"

Mrs. Clifford felt unable to return to her home after this bereavement; she decided to remain abroad until the time when it would be necessary for Herbert to return for his studies at college. Herbert worked diligently with his tutor; but the Book he loved the best was his father's Greek Testament—his father's constant companion in the last years of his life, and his pa·ting gift to Herbert. With this he would wander forth before his mother's time of rising, while the early morning glowed in rose and purple on the snowy mountain heights and the overhanging clouds, winding along through the steep mountain-path ; or, when evening fell, seated in the Swiss peasant's lowly chalet, reading of the "Lamb of God who taketh away the sin of the world." Then again in some boat of transport on lake or river, while his mother yielded herself to the calm influence of Earth and Sky, as they glided on between the blue water below and bluer Heaven above, Herbert with the same Book of Life—the same small Book his hand could cover, but whose span is infinite, and date eternal—with that wondrous Book, Herbert would talk to the benighted sailors, or the travelling peasants, or not seldom to some company of Romish priests, winning the hearts of even those whose spiritual fetters he could not break, till sometimes the young priest would take his leave with his arms encircling the neck of his gentle but dauntless opponent. Thus passed away Herbert's early youth, while he gazed intently on the volume of Nature's beauty; the volume of man's recorded thoughts; and the volume of Divine Inspiration.

VI.

The Farmer's Sacrifice.

"Pure religion, and undefiled before God and the Father, is this, To visit the fatherless and widows in their affliction, and to keep himself unspotted from the world."—James, i. 27.

"Why should we fear, youth's draught of joy
If pure, would sparkle less?
Why should the cup the sooner cloy,
Which God hath deigned to bless?"

The arrival of the curate in the village was a subject of great interest, and tended more than any other event probably could have done, to alleviate the sorrow felt on the departure of the Squire's family. Many there were who went to Church on the first Sunday, in expectation and hope; and among these was little Rose; her face gathered brightness when the prayers were read with fervent distinctness; but as the new Minister preached, it became beaming with joy; and no sooner had they passed the Church's door, than Rose exclaimed, "O, father! that is just like our Minister at school, that is exactly how he preaches; O I am so glad! Did you not like that, father?"

"Yes, dear, I could sit all day to hear such

M. C.

words as those! I thank God he is come in my time!"

Mrs. Smith had hastened on before with a still quicker step than usual, and when Rose reached home with her father, her mother was already preparing the dinner. If Rose had looked at her mother's face she would have seen no pleased expression there, but she was too full of delight to question the possibility of any one feeling different; so she ran in to the family kitchen, and exclaimed at once, "O, mother! was not that beautiful preaching? That was just like our Minister at school!"

"I am sure I don't know," replied Mrs. Smith; "it may be beautiful enough for some, but certainly not for me!"

"Did you not like it then, mother?"

"Like it, child? I don't know who would like to be told that when they have done their best, and lived respected as I have, and always kept their church, that for all that they must turn and seek the same way to Heaven as the worst of sinners!"

"Oh, mother, that is because our Saviour is 'the way,' as the minister said in his text."

"Well, child, I don't know as to what the way may be, I only know I have lived a very different life from many, and I don't choose to be mixed up with them, as if I were the same as they!"

"But, mother, it's because our Saviour is the only way to Heaven, and every one must come to Him who wants to go to Heaven; and He can take all their sins away! Miss Clifford said she wanted to come to Jesus our Saviour!"

"Well, child, that might be, for Miss Clifford never did seem to consider herself above the lowest; for my part, I can't come to that; but I don't mean to talk about it; there is no need for you to change your mind, nor I mine!"

Rose said no more, her sudden joy was dashed as suddenly with disappointment. From this time Mrs. Smith made a point of never going to church when she knew the curate would preach; her temper became more trying to all around her; and if it had not been for the comfort of the Sunday's sermons, Rose and her father would have found it hard to keep up their spirits through the week.

What was pain to Mrs. Smith, was not only comfort to Rose and her father, it was also joy to old Willy. Twice on the Sabbath-day the old man climbed the hill supported by his staff, and the glad sound was always new life to him. The weekly visits also of the curate were his delight; but he always questioned him as to whether any tidings had been heard of his young master; and he said it was a heart-affecting thing that he, an old man as he was, should live to see the young and good pass clear away like that—one taken up above, and the other into foreign parts! But when at last a letter came to the curate, and a message in it to old Willy, written with Herbert's own hand all those miles away, joy lighted up the old man's eye, and he exclaimed, " Who can tell, but I shall see him yet again before I die!" The faithful Jem seemed to consider old Willy now as his peculiar charge; scarcely a day passed that he did not look in at the cottage. The little plot of garden-ground he took under his entire care—there, early and late, was heard his busy spade; it was Jem who dug up and stowed under ground the bright red potatoes, to protect them from the frost; Jem, who managed to buy the old man's coals at less cost in the town, and brought them back in a return wagon of farmer Smith's; Jem, who when the snow had melted, planted in the early vegetables; tended the flowers as spring came on; cut the garden hedge; and trained the vine above the lattice-window; in short, Jem, the old man said, tended him like a prince. Little Mercy, too, would often step up to the cottage and find out work the old man wanted done; when his sight was dim, she would read to him; and sometimes she would take her knitting up and sit and sing to him. Thus was old Willy tended still and comforted.

A year and six months had passed away since

William left his home, and he had not been down once to visit it. His father had written in the autumn, and written again at Christmas, to ask him to come; but William returned for answer that he could see no prospect yet of doing anything for his brothers, nor therefore of returning himself to live at home; and that till he did, he could not trust himself to come, for fear he should lose his resolution, and not return to his work in London any more. But he sent his love to his mother, and he hoped to sow and reap again with his father for her; his love to Joe and Samson, and he still hoped to make great men of them; his love to Ted, and the first good berth he could find on board ship should be his—if he would learn well at school; his love to little Tim, and he would come home some day and teach him to plough, and till then Tim was to be sure and take care of Black Beauty; and finally his love to Rose, and she must come up and see him in London: and so, wishing a happy Christmas to them all, ended William's second Christmas letter.

When the spring-time came, tidings arrived in the village of the death of the Squire, and the continued residence of his lady and her son abroad. The loss was much felt, for the Squire was greatly beloved; and it was all the more felt because his affairs were left in such perfect order, that no tenant's sense of the loss of a friend was turned into anxiety as to personal concerns; all felt that a friend and counsellor was gone, and felt it still the more, from the tokens of care for their interest and comfort which the communications received made evident. Old Willy mourned the loss, and doubted now that he should never live to see his own young master any more!

The hay-time was scarcely over, when an invitation came to Rose from her uncle in London to pay him a visit. Rose was much pleased with the thought of going to London; but her chief joy was the prospect of seeing William. Mr. Smith's brother in London, Mr. Samson Smith, lived in a country-house, some few miles out of the great city. William met Rose at the inn where the coach stopped, and took her down to her uncle's house. There seemed to Rose no end of streets or people, but she had few thoughts for them—her joy at sight of her brother swallowed up all beside. Her uncle's house was very different from her home; there was a carpet all over the floor, paintings round the room, a pier-glass over the mantel-piece, and more than one sofa. Her aunt and cousins were very kind to her, and her uncle also; yet Rose felt strange, and when William went away in the evening she could hardly keep from crying. But in a few days she was more at home; and her aunt took Rose into London with her cousins, and showed her some of the sights that make the great city famous—Rose saw the wild beasts; she also saw the Tower, where, in days gone by, so many a noble prisoner heard the key turn that separated between him and all he loved on Earth—for ever! Rose saw the river with its forest of masts; she saw the streets again, and wondered how they could be all full of people at once; but she saw nothing like her own sweet woods and fields, no rippling stream, no shading trees, no free bird warbling praise; and she began to think about the time when she should go home again. She saw but little of William; he could seldom get down, except on Sundays, and then she could not talk much to him, before her aunt and cousins.

Had the ministering child nothing to do for others away from her home? O, yes! we have always something to do for others, and something to learn, wherever we may be. Rose tried to be useful to her aunt and cousins, but they were all happy, and did not seem really to want her; her uncle was very kind to her, but he never seemed to want her; the servants were attentive to her, but they looked well satisfied. William could seldom come; and Rose thought of her own village far away—she knew that there were many who wanted her there; some of the poor old people wanted her, she knew; and her father must miss her sadly, and little Tim, and her mother also—

and Rose felt that she would be rather where she was really WANTED, than seeing all the fine sights in the world. Was there no one then who wanted Rose where she was gone to stay? You will hear.

One day, in her aunt's house, Rose heard a tale of sorrow. A poor man, a workman in a brewery near, had fallen into one of the great beer-vats, and been killed. He had left a wife and three little children, to live on Earth without him, and the poor woman's heart was almost broken with her sorrow. A kind lady went round to collect a little money, that a mangle might be bought, for the poor widow to earn her bread, and Rose's aunt gave some money to help. The next day Rose heard the servants talking about this same poor woman, so she asked the housemaid about her, and the housemaid said, "While they are collecting this money, the poor thing is almost dying of distress and want!" "But don't they go and see her, and take her some of it?" asked Rose. "No, they are keeping it all to do something to get her a living with; and she is so distracted with grief that no one likes to go and see her!" Rose said no more that day, but she thought in her heart that the love of Jesus could comfort any sorrow, and that if no one else would go, she ought to try and comfort the poor widow. So she asked the housemaid where the poor woman lived; and the next time she was out alone, she had to pass the end of the little path that led up to her cottage; Rose thought it might be terrible to see such grief, but it must be worse to bear it and have no comforter, so she turned up the narrow pathway that led to the house; she thought if she could not comfort her she could give her some money she had, that would buy her food for a little while; so she went. She knocked at the door, and some one said, "Come in!" Rose lifted the latch, and went in. There stood the poor woman, looking very pale, as if she had cried for days and nights.

"I am so sorry for you!" said Rose. The poor woman sat down, and wiped away her tears with her apron; and Rose sat by her and talked to her of Jesus, and the poor woman listened to all Rose had to say, and took what Rose had brought for her, and was as gentle as the ministering child herself. Then Rose went away, and she saw there was no need to be afraid of sorrow when we go to it in the name of JESUS. It was the poor widow, with none to visit her, who wanted Rose.

William had to go some distance on business for his uncle; he was away several days, and when he returned, the time had come for Rose to go back to her home. William came down quite early one morning to take her into London to the coach; and as soon as he was alone with Rose in

ROSE'S VISIT TO THE WIDOW IN LONDON.

Ministering Children. Vol. II, p 92.

the Fly he said, "Rose, I have a secret I will tell you, if you promise not to tell father, or mother, or any one, till I write about it." Rose promised not to tell, and William talked earnestly to her, and Rose listened, all anxiety, till the Fly stopped at the inn. Then William put Rose into the coach, and as he leaned on the door, he said, "Oh! I would give all I have earned, to be going back with you, if it was only myself I had to think of!" And then charging Rose once more to keep the secret, the coach drove off, and Rose soon lost sight of William at the turning of the street, while full of joy she looked forward to her home. It was a long day's journey; but when the coach stopped at the little village inn nearest to her home, to change horses, there stood her father, and the horse in the gig, waiting for her. Very joyful was the meeting between Rose and her father. "And what of poor Will?" said her father, when Rose was seated by his side in the gig, and they had started for home—"what of poor Will?"

"Oh! he wished so he could come with me!" replied Rose, "I could not bear to leave him!"

"Poor boy!" said farmer Smith, "I doubt we must have him home after all; he will never settle, so far from the place!"

"No, father, he would not live in London always, for any money! but he would not leave it now, I know, for he says he shall stay till he has worked out a way for the young ones,—all except Tim, he says he never could part with Tim, and he knows that if he can only get back in time enough to teach Tim farming, that he will take to it better than anything else, and I am sure Tim is more like William than any of them."

"Well, I don't know, I am sure," said farmer Smith, "but these are not times to settle boys out in a day; and I am sure I would not be the father to keep a son like him pining away from his home, seeking after what may never be found."

"O father, Will does not pine! Why he is grown into such a man as you would never believe—and as busy as anything. I wish you could see him; and I know a secret, father, only I am not to tell you or any one, so you won't say anything, will you, father?"

Farmer Smith looked down anxiously on his child's bright face, but she did not perceive the anxiety of the look; she thought if the subject-matter of a secret were not revealed, the fact of its existence must be a lawful and interesting communication; so she went on to say, "It's only good, father; and if it comes to be, then you, and mother, and all will know it; but I promised Will not to tell!" And Rose thought she was only giving hope and pleasure by her intimation of the existence of a secret—for how should her inexperienced childhood understand a parent's anxious questioning!

Chesnut in the gig trotted swiftly along, and Rose soon gave a shout at sight of her home—with its white vine-covered walls, its sheltering barns and stacks; and then the yard-boy driving Fillpail, and Cowslip, and Rosebud, and all their companions back from their milking to their pasture in the valley. And then her brothers caught sight of the gig, and ran out with their welcome, and little Tim came trotting after them; and at the door stood their mother, in her afternoon gown of red-patterned print, and Rose thought how nice she looked; and how fresh and sweet and clean all seemed, after the London suburbs and the dingy city she had left.

When all were seated at tea, Joe and the little sprightly Ted began their questioning, and Rose with no less animation replied. At last Joe said, "Well, I suppose William begins to find out that there is something better to be done, than walking backwards and forwards over a field after a plough all the days of one's life?"

"O no!" exclaimed Rose indignantly, "he says there is nothing he counts on more than the day when he shall lace on his plough-boots again on father's farm!"

"Poor boy! poor boy!" said farmer Smith. "I am sure there is nothing I count on like having him back again for good!"

"Why then did you ever let him go?" asked Mrs. Smith. "You know it was all your doing If I had had my way, he never should have set his foot in London; by what I hear they have people enough, and too many, up there as it is, and why we should be sending our best off to them—I never did, and I never shall see the reason of!"

"Well, wife," said farmer Smith sorrowfully, "it seemed as if it might be for the best in the end; but I am sure I don't know; and if we have not One above to order for us, I don't know who is to tell what is for the best! It's certain I thought I should get over the loss of him better than I have."

"I don't suppose you thought about how you would get over it at all!" replied Mrs. Smith, "it never was your way; when you take a thing up, you are for doing it—and then let the feeling come after as it may! I could have told you that you would never get over the loss of him, only you would not have minded it if I had!"

Farmer Smith made no further remark during tea, and as soon as it was over he took his hat and went out into his farm, to relieve his burdened spirit with the freshness of the evening air. And while the boys made haste to help their mother clear the tea-table, Rose slipped away after her father, and with her hand in his soon dispersed the gloom that had gathered on his face.

"I wish enough," said Joe that evening to Rose, "that I had not said anything about William at tea, mother always takes it up so, and then it vexes father! I only know, I wish I could go to London, too, for it is as dull as dullness always to be walking over the same fields, and see no one but the same ten heavy men all the days of one's life; I am sure I can't think how father can stand it, only I suppose he likes it! Did William say anything about me?"

Rose hesitated a little, Joe' squick eye turned instantly at her silence, and fixed upon her. "He said," replied Rose, "that he was sure you would not like uncle's shop any better than farming."

"No, so I told him," replied Joe. "I don't see any more spirit in laying up and taking down bales of goods, and cutting yards of stuffs, than in putting in turnips and then taking them out again, and cutting them up for the sheep—all over and over year after year! What I should like would be a merchant's office, where some day I might travel, and not have only what grows at one's door to do with all the days of one's life! Did Will say anything about that?"

"He said," replied Rose, "that he would never give up trying after it; for he did not believe that, so much as you had read and thought about it, you would ever settle to anything else."

"What a good fellow he is!" said Joe, "he al

ways did seem to care as much about what one felt as what one did oneself—let it be the least thing in the world even. If ever he makes a merchant of me, he shall see what a memory I have for things I have heard him say, and what I will get hold of and do to please him! I wish I was off, for there's no getting on here, all one tries to do seems to go for nothing, as to making any real difference. Just think what it would be to work one's way up there and buy this farm for father, instead of every now and then hearing it is likely to be sold over his head; or pay the rent for him; or anything to keep off that harass that's always upon him; but somehow there seems no getting on, and no spirit in anything here!"

"Oh, Joe, the spirit is not in THINGS, the spirit is in US! I have heard William say that you may PUT spirit into anything! And he thinks there's nothing like farming, for the pleasure of it."

"Well, I am sure father never finds fault with me, but William said it was hard to settle to work you cannot get a liking for!"

"So I dare say it is," replied Rose, "but only you try and be a comfort to father, and see if William does not soon find you something up in London!"

Joe took the assurance of sympathy and hope, and went the next morning with fresh spirit to work.

Rose was often seen looking out from door or

window about the morning hour of ten, and when she saw the postman climbing the green ascent to her home, she would run out to receive what he had brought, but she still always returned with slower steps—no letter from William was there! At length, one baking morning, when Rose was busy in the back-kitchen making the harvest-cakes, farmer Smith called Mrs. Smith and Rose into the parlor, where he stood with an open letter in his hand. The heart of Rose beat quick, for she guessed that the secret had come at last! Farmer Smith shut the parlour door, saying, "Here is a letter from Will, and no time to be lost in attending to it!" so saying, he read as follows:—

DEAR FATHER,

I hope I have gathered my first sheaf, after pretty near a two years' waiting for it; but I have again and again thought how you used to say, when I wanted to be hasty in housing the crops, "Waiting time is often the time that pays best in the end!" Well, father, I told Rose a bit of a secret, but she promised to keep it, so I may as well tell you and mother from the beginning. You know how Joe has always been bent on a merchant's office. I was so certain nothing else would content him that I always kept that in my eye, but I never got so much as the least prospect, or chance of trying for him. Well, a week before Rose went home I had to go a journey on business for my uncle; there was an elderly gentleman seated by me outside the coach, and we had not gone far when a terrible thunder-shower came on. I had an umbrella, for I had seen a threatening of it; the old gentleman had none, and he was seated at the end just where the storm beat, so I said, "If you will please to change places, sir, I could shelter you better in the middle here." At that he looked up, and said, "I am sure you are very good to say so, but I have no right to expect shelter from you, and an old man ought to be better provided against a storm than a young one—don't you consider so?" "Well, sir," I said, "I don't know but what the young have quite as much reason to look out as the old!" By this the old gentleman had changed his place, but he soon began to call out that I was getting his share of the storm. "I am no way afraid of that, sir," said I, "I have been used to stand a shower all my days." "How is that?" he asked. "Well, sir, I was brought up to the farming, and you can't be a farmer and afraid of a shower! but a soaking is dangerous sometimes, when you are not used to it." Then the old gentleman put no end of questions to me, and I found he knew pretty well about farming himself; he told me he was born and brought up on a farm, and certainly he pleased me better than any one I had met all the time I have been in London—near enough now upon two years. In all that time uncle Samson has never asked me half so many questions about you, and the farm, and the boys, as that old gentleman did that day, and all as if he cared to know! it did me more good than any talk I had had since I left home. The old gentleman gave me his card at the end of the journey, and told me to call on him as soon as I returned to London, for he was going to return the next day. I found by his card that he lived not very far from my uncle's, and when I showed it to him, he told me that he knew him well by name, and that he was a man of excellent standing, a merchant in London. O, how I thought of Joe—and what if after all this should be the making of him! I went down the very first evening to see him; he seemed to be living alone by what I could make out, in a beautiful house, and certainly he was one of the pleasantest persons I ever spoke to; he remembered every word I had told him, and there I sat talking to him, just as if I had been at home. Well, it so happened that Joe being so much on my mind, I had told all about him outside the coach, before ever I knew what the old gentleman was, and how glad I was to think I had, for I should not have liked to speak about it then, I could not have done it half so well! The old gentleman never said a word of what I was so full of hope about, and when I went away I thought all was over, for he only said he should hope to see me again some day. Well, two days ago what should come but a note from him to invite me to dine with him! And then he told me that he had called on my uncle, and satisfied himself as far as he could, that he was not venturing too much—and that he now offered me a situation in his office for my younger brother, provided he proved capable on trial. "But," said he, "my premium is a hundred pounds; I require two hundred with the sons of gentlemen, and have never taken any with less: do you think your father can provide that sum?" Well, I would not for anything put a hindrance in the way, so I said, I hoped that might not be found to stand in the way of so excellent an offer. Then the old gentleman seemed satisfied; and I should have been sorry not to give Joe as good a start as we could, and pay him regularly in: and as I dare say the old gentleman knows my uncle is rich, it might have looked encroaching on the kindness of his offer, if I had made any difficulty. So now at last the thing is settled. But for the money—take my advice, father, and do not worry to think it over yourself, for I have thought it all over and over again, and there is but one way—and that way will soon do it. First, then, I have thirty pounds all ready at once, saved out of these two years; then, to meet the rest, there is but one thing to be done—Black Beauty must be sold; don't keep vexing about it, father; but let it be done, and you will never repent it. I say the more because I know you will think most about me in selling him; but I have made up my mind, and it would hurt me a great deal more to have any difficulty in Joe's way with such an offer as this. Tell mother not to vex about the horse. I can rear another such, some day, when I am your farming-man again: he ought to fetch seventy pounds to say the least, but if you cannot get that at hands likely to do well by him, then you can make up the rest without much difficulty, by selling off what remains of last year's wheat. Let me decide for you, father, as I think I best can in this case, because I know the value of the offer. You must have Joe and the money ready in a fortnight; and then tell mother when I have seen Joe settled, I will come home for a holiday. My love to all, and good wishes to Joe.

Your affectionate Son, WILLIAM SMITH.

P. S.—At first I thought I would make an effort and ask my uncle to lend me the seventy pounds, but then I remembered what you have so often said to me—"Bear anything rather than borrow, Will!" So I did not ask my uncle, and I dare say he supposes we can easily raise the money, for he never inquires much as to how farming stands.

"O, father," exclaimed Rose, "that's the secret! May I run and tell Joe?"

"And what do you mean to do?" asked Mrs. Smith of her husband.

"Well, I suppose we can't do better than take William's advice; these are no times to bring up five boys on one small farm, and Joe has no mind to the work."

"I," said Mrs. Smith, "always found I must put my mind in my work, and then my work came to my mind, and I have trained Rose to the same; but, as I always said, you must rule the boys: only don't let me see the horse led away—that is all I have to say!" and Mrs. Smith returned to the back-kitchen. Rose stayed by her father's side—what would he have done but for his little comforter! "Never mind, father, never mind!" she said. "It's sure to be right if Will says so, you know it always is!"

"Then you think it had better be as William says?" asked the father of his little daughter.

"O, yes, father; William must know better up there—among so many people, than we do down here; only mother never likes things different, but she will be glad some day! May I go and tell Joe now?"

"Yes, if you like. Your mother's taking things so contrary, makes them a heavy burden! I am sure I am sorry enough for the poor beast; but it's better than borrowing!"

Farmer Smith took his hat; and Rose ran to

look for Joe. She found him busy in the fields among the men; so calling him on one side, she told him all, except about the horse. Joe rushed to the house wild with joy. The first person he met was his mother.

"O mother! I am to be a merchant after all! William has found me a place in London!"

"Well, I can't help it!" said Mrs. Smith.

"No, mother, I don't want it helped! it's the thing of all others I have most wished for!"

"And what is the use of never being satisfied in one place, till you are in another, I should like to know?" asked Mrs. Smith. "There's William always sighing after his home, and I dare say you will like London no better!"

"Why, mother, Will never did like it; he always said it was only for us he went away; but it's the very thing I have always longed for, so I am sure to like it!"

"Well, I only hope it may be so!" replied Mrs. Smith; and Joe went off to look for warmer sympathy in his father. He did not look in vain; but after some conversation, farmer Smith said, "I am sorry for the horse; but it cannot be helped!"

"What horse, father?"

"Did not Rose tell you? We must sell Black Beauty, to pay the premium."

"Sell Black Beauty, father! no, that you must

not; William would never bear the sight of me, if his horse had been sold to get me up there; I would sooner not go!" And the lad's voice faltered with struggling feelings.

"Yes, but it is William himself who says so!" replied his father.

"Does William say so?" asked Joe. "Well, I never thought he could have given up so much for me!"

Now it happened that the old clergyman had long taken a great fancy to Black Beauty, as a fine horse for his hooded carriage; and he had more than once asked farmer Smith to let him know if ever he thought of parting with it; so, acting on his son William's advice, farmer Smith lost no time in calling on the Rector. The old clergyman seemed pleased with a prospect of possessing the horse, but said that he had fixed the price that he would give, namely fifty pounds, beyond which he would not go. Farmer Smith stated that the horse was worth more; that he felt no doubt a dealer would give him more; that it was only a sudden necessity he could not meet, compelled him to sell the horse; but that he greatly desired to secure a good master for him. Now the old clergyman was rich, and had no children, but he made no inquiry as to why the horse had to be sold; he only said, "I have stated the price I will give; you must take it or not, as seems best to you." Farmer Smith sat a few minutes in harassed thought; he wished his little Rose had been at his side, to say one way or the other; at last, feeling for the creature outweighed the hope of a larger price, and he replied, "Well, sir, I would sooner let him go for less to a good master, than strain a point and get a bad one. The horse is worth full seventy pounds, but as I am driven to it by necessity, I will take the fifty for him, if you please, sir."

"Very well," said the old clergyman; "I gave fifty pounds for the best horse I ever had, and I never mean to give more, or I may probably get a worse!" So farmer Smith took the offer, and the horse was to be fetched away the next day.

It was late in the afternoon when the Rector's coachman came for the horse. Ted saw him coming, and gave the alarm, then ran off to the stable to give Black Beauty his last supper. Joe followed slowly, and Rose with him, trying to cheer him; but he took his stand, pale and silent, within the stable, half concealed from view. Samson stood with great composure at the farm-yard gate, watching the approach of the man; while little Tim, hearing from Molly what was about to happen, came running and crying as he ran, and lisping out in sobs, "No, no, naughty man! Back Booty not go! Will said, 'Tim, take care of Back Booty!'" Ted had filled a measure of the brim, and the high and gentle creature stooped his head to feed; but when little Tim came sobbing in, the creature turned from its food, looked hard at the child, and then stooped down its face to him, as if to caress and soothe.

Farmer Smith and the coachman soon entered. Farmer Smith looked on the group one moment in silent feeling almost as strong as his children's, then stroking down his favourite's silky mane, he said, "There's the horse; I give him to you in good condition, and a better horse you cannot find."

"I am sorry for you, sir!" said the coachman; and farmer Smith left the stable, unable to stay and witness the scene.

"You will let him get his supper first?" said Ted, looking up, and holding the measure afresh to Black Beauty's head.

"Go, naughty man, go quite away!" said little Tim, "Will shall be very angry with you!" and the horse turned from his food again to the child.

"Come now, Tim," said Ted, "you won't let him have a bit of supper!" and Tim suffered Rose to compose and comfort him while Black Beauty eat his food; but the moment it was done and the halter was in the coachman's hand, Tim's grief broke forth again, while Ted, and Rose, and Joe, at that sight, no longer kept from tears. The man tried to make short work of it, and lead the horse at once away, but the creature threw up his head; his eye that had looked so mildly on the child, grew fierce, and snorting he seemed to bid the stranger defiance in his attempt to secure and lead him away. Then Joe looked up in blank distress, and said, "It's of no use, he won't go for you, a stranger never led him! Give him to me, it's fit I should have to lead him away, for it's all for me has to go!" So Joe took the halter, the creature hung down his head and followed, and the children followed also—little Tim stamping with impotent distress. The heavy-laden wagon coming in at the stack-yard gate stood still, and the men looked round to watch; and the labourers, winding up the hill with their rakes upon their shoulders, turned to see the faithful creature go, and Molly and the yard-boy stood in view, and Mrs. Smith within the house kept up a more than usual stir, and farmer Smith—no one knew where he was. Rose soon stopped with little Tim; but Ted ran on by the side of Joe, who led the horse to his new stable, then the boys threw their arms around his neck, and left him to his new abode; and long Black Beauty neighed in vain for the children's hands to feed him.

"Never mind, my boy!" said farmer Smith, as Joe turned away from his supper, "You won't trifle with a situation that has cost us all so much!"

"What in the world is this?" asked Mrs. Smith, as she packed her son Joe's box for London.

"O, never mind, mother, just tuck it in anywhere."

"But what in the world is it for?" asked Mrs. Smith.

"Well, mother, it's only just the old bit of rope with which I led Black Beauty away; he would not let the Rector's man halter him or lead him out of the stable!"

"And what can be the use of taking that?" asked Mrs. Smith.

"O, never mind, mother—only for fear I should ever forget that day!"

"Well, I am sure," said Mrs. Smith, "it's an odd fancy—to hold feeling by a bit of old rope! but so it must be if you will."

Perhaps Mrs. Smith was really more capable of understanding Joe's feelings than she shewed signs of being; Black Beauty's old bit of rope was tucked in the corner of the box; and Joe went to London, and the merchant was pleased with the lad, and the money was paid, and William took Joe to lodge with him; and when he had seen him comfortably settled, William went down to spend a fortnight in his home—to the comfort of all, and not least of little Tim. And Black Beauty drew the Minister's carriage.

VII.

Little Jane's Carpet.

"Warmed underneath the Comforter's safe wing,
They spread th' endearing warmth around."

"Putting on the breast-plate of faith and love."—1 Thess. v. 8.

WHILE these events had been passing in the village, little Jane had followed on her childhood's path within the town; and the energy of growing thought, and the courage of deepening feeling, strengthened within her heart. Her sympathy for the Poor grew with her growth—a sympathy inherited by birth from her parents, and constantly nourished by the atmosphere of her home; a respectful sympathy; a loving feeling of relationship; a sense of some invisible tie existing between her and the Poor, which did not exist between her and the Rich—even that most blessed bond, the power to aid and comfort!

There was a road which led out of the town, on the side nearest to Mr. Mansfield's house; the road led up a long hill, and then crossed a wide heath; this was a favourite walk with Jane and her little brothers, and here they used to run, and

and play with the snow, in the winter time, to which we have now come;—while William and Joe were together in London, little Mercy and her uncle Jem tending old Willy, Herbert away in a foreign land, Rose busy in her home, and Black Beauty drawing the Minister's carriage. There on the fresh-blowing heath, Jane and her little brothers grew rosy with their play. Scattered cottages and huts stood upon this open heath, and Jane often stopped in her play and looked at them, or passed them by with slower step—she felt that the Poor were there! There was one hut that stood separated from any other, a mean abode it was, and with no look of comfort round it; there was a pile of turf to lengthen out the smouldering fire, but no little stack of wood, no black and shining coal, no cheerful blaze within. No Herbert came and went that way; no faithful Jem lived near; but little Jane's eye of thoughtful love—so early trained to watch where any want might rest—her eye of thoughtful love had marked the mean abode, and again and again she had looked, wondering who might live there! At last, one wintry day, just as Jane passed by, the door opened, and an aged woman came out with a ragged cloth in her hand, which she hung on a snowy bramble that grew before the door. The aged woman wore an old print gown, with a small black shawl pinned over her shoulders, and an old black bonnet on her head; her head shook with the palsy of age, and it was evident at first sight that she was very old, and very poor.

"Look, nurse," said Jane, "that poor old woman lives there!"

"Yes, I see," said nurse.

"Do you think mamma knows that old woman?" asked Jane.

"How can I tell," replied nurse, "you don't suppose your mamma knows every old woman for miles round the town?"

Nurse was walking at a quick pace with the little boys, and she called to Jane, who was lingering with her eyes still on the open cottage door, to come on; so Jane hastened on. As they returned, the aged woman stood outside her door again, putting out a few more ragged things to dry on the bushes in the wintry wind. Jane watched her as she passed, but said no more to her nurse. As soon as she was alone with her mother that day, she said, "Mamma, what do you think! I saw such a very old woman in such a very old cottage; she looked so cold, and her head shook, and she was hanging out some ragged things to dry, and I saw no fire inside! Do you know her, mamma?"

"Where did you see her?" asked Mrs. Mansfield.

"Out on the heath, mamma; such a very old

cottage—alone by itself! I am sure she is very poor, and she must be very cold."

"I don't think I know anything of her," replied Mrs. Mansfield; "but if you think she is so very old and poor, you shall take me to see her, and then we shall both know her!"

"O, mamma, will you let me? shall we go this afternoon?"

"No; you could not walk so far twice in one day."

"O, yes, I could indeed, mamma, I am not at all tired!"

"No, we will wait till to-morrow, and then if the day is very fine I will promise, if possible to go with you."

"Shall you do anything to make her warm, mamma?"

"Yes; if you like we will take her a coal-ticket, and then she will be able to have some coals."

"O, mamma, I am so glad! I wish I could do something for her as well!"

"We will observe, when we go, what she seems most to want, and then perhaps you can take it to her some day in your walk with nurse."

"Do you mean I may go in, all alone by myself, mamma?"

"Yes, if she seems a kind old woman, who would be pleased to have a little visitor."

"Are not all poor people kind, then, mamma?"

"No, dear Jane, not all; an evil heart within them makes some poor people unkind and wicked, as it does some rich people. And then the poor often suffer a great deal; and when they have not the fear and love of God to comfort them, suffering often makes them speak and feel and act as they would not, if they knew the love of God."

"Cannot they be taught to know it, then, mamma?"

"Yes, Jane, we must try to help every one to know the love of God, through Jesus Christ. God's love can change the hardest and most wicked heart, and make it gentle and patient—even in suffering. So when we find any one unkind to us, whether poor or rich, we must try and show them what the love of God can teach and enable us to bear and to do; and if we can we must tell them of His love, that they may seek it also."

"If the old woman is unkind, what will you do, mamma?"

"I do not think she will be; but if she should, we must speak the more gently and kindly to her, and perhaps she will soon find that we only want to be a help and comfort to her, and then she will be glad to see us; and our love may lead her to seek the love of God—and that will make her happy in her poor cottage here, and then it will take her to Heaven!"

Jane was satisfied, and asked no more; she had learned an added lesson of truth; no suspicion had been taught her; her mother had only reminded her of the fact—that from sin's evil root we must not be surprised to find its bitter fruit; and she had bound upon her child "the breast-plate of faith and love," to shield her from the painful effects of a surprise. The youngest soldier of the cross needs to be so prepared and guarded, when venturing on ground untried by others for his steps; and care is needed—is greatly needed, lest the older mind teach caution by infusing suspicion and doubt; instead of giving the simple knowledge of the universal fact that man's heart is evil, and carefully binding on the child's young spirit that breast-plate of FAITH and LOVE which can alone guard it for its safe conflict with the world.

The next day Jane set off with her mother for the cottage on the heath. It was true she walked with more silent questionings—as to what they might meet in the old woman's cottage,—but it was the questioning that belongs to Earth's uncertainty; and whatever might be found, she was prepared to meet it now, without being driven back by a surprise. The cottage-door was shut; on Mrs. Mansfield's knocking, the old woman opened it, and Mrs. Mansfield said, "We have walked up from the town to call on you, may we come in?"

"It's no place to come into," said the aged woman, "but you can if you like!"

Mrs. Mansfield went in, and sat down on a broken chair; Jane found a seat on the bottom of the bedstead, and the aged woman sat down again by her small table, where she was taking her twelve o'clock dinner of a little tea and a crust of bread.

"You must feel the cold on this open heath!" said Mrs. Mansfield.

"Yes, it's enough to perish an old woman like me; but I could never make up the high rent down in the town, so I am forced to bear it as I can!"

"We thought that you might like a coal-ticket; they are giving some in the town, do you know about them?"

"Oh, yes! I know about them."

"Would you like to have one?"

"Well, I can have it if you like, but I don't suppose I can ever get the coals out here; I am sure I can't carry them!"

"No, you would not carry them yourself; but I see some other cottages near; perhaps you have a neighbour who could?"

"No, there's no one who neighbours with me; I have no one to look to but myself; what I can do for myself I do, and what I can't I have to go without."

"Could you manage if you had a shilling with it? Then you could pay the sixpence that is necessary with the ticket, and give something to a boy to carry them for you."

"Yes, I suppose I could do that!"

"Shall I write your name on the ticket then? I have a pen and ink in my basket."

"You can, if you please."

So Mrs. Mansfield wrote; then turning to the aged woman, she said, "You feel as if you had no one to look to; but there is a Friend who is able and willing to help and comfort you, if you ask it of Him."

"I suppose you mean there is a God above," said the old woman; "I know that!"

"I mean that the God above sent His beloved Son to die for you, that you might find pardon, and help, and hope in Him—even in Jesus the Son of God."

"Well, I dare say it may be; but those who have no learning like me cannot come at the understanding of it."

"Oh, yes, you can, by God's help! It is to the Poor that the good news is sent. It is all written in the Bible for you, and if you only get its words into your heart, they are sure to lead you to heaven."

"I can't do that then, for I can't read them; and I am not fit to go to a place of worship."

"Oh yes, you are quite fit for that; there are many who have worshipped God in worse clothing than yours! But if you like, my little girl shall come and read to you sometimes, when she walks this way?"

"Well, I am for the most part busy."

"Never mind; if you are busy she can run on with her brothers; but if you are not busy she can come and read the words of the Bible to you—those blessed words that are written for the Poor!"

"I am sure you are very good!" said the old woman, softened at last. And Mrs. Mansfield and Jane took their leave.

"She was not really unkind, was she, mamma?" asked Jane, anxious to clear as much as possible any censure from her old woman.

"No, dear, she was not at all unkind, only very poor and very miserable; and when people are very miserable, they often don't feel able to speak pleasantly."

"No, mamma: do you think she will like me to read to her?"

"Yes, I feel sure she will after a little time. I think she will soon begin to love you, Jane; and perhaps you may teach her to know the love of God her Saviour; then she will feel very different, and look very different."

"Shall I go to-morrow, mamma?"

"No, I dare say she will go for her coals to-morrow; you had better wait a day or two, and perhaps by that time she will begin to look out for your promised visit."

"I saw something she wanted, mamma; did you?"

"Yes, poor old woman! I thought she wanted almost everything!"

"But I mean her tea-pot, mamma; did you see it was tied together with a string?"

"No, I did not see that."

"It was indeed, mamma! How much would a tea-pot cost?"

"You could get a small black tea-pot for six-pence."

"Six weeks then, mamma, it would take me before I could buy one!"

"Yes, it would; but you need not wait for that, because I think I have a tea-pot at home I could spare; it is a pewter tea-pot, a good deal bent, but it has no holes in it."

"May I take it then, mamma, when I go?"

"Yes, and if you like, you shall make her a warm garment, and take it to her as a present from me." So Jane, with delight, gave her play-time to work, till in three days the warm garment was read; then, with the tea-pot packed in a basket, and a little tea and sugar from her father beside it, and with her mother's warm present tied up in a parcel, the happy child set forth with her brothers and her nurse. O, how she longed to reach the cottage! And when at last it came in sight, she said, "Nurse, may I run on now?" and then swiftly she crossed the wintry heath, and knocked at the old woman's door.

"O, it's you!" said the old woman; "I have looked out for you!"

"Mamma has sent you this!" said Jane, unfolding her mother's present; "will it not keep you warm? I made it for you all myself, except the fixing!"

"I never had the like of it before!" said the old woman with evident surprise.

"And mamma said I might bring you this teapot," said Jane; "and there is some tea and sugar from our shop!"

"I am sure you are very good to me!" said the old woman, with feeling in her tone.

"Are you busy to-day?" asked Jane.

"No, I am not busy, I have nothing to be busy about!"

"Shall I stay a little while?"

"Yes, dear, if you can content yourself."

"O yes, I like to stay with you, you must be so dull here all alone! Do you like me to read to you? I have brought my own Bible!"

"As you please," replied the old woman.

"I can read to you about Heaven, in the Revelation," said Jane; and she read from the 7th chapter of Revelation, the 9th verse to the end of the chapter.

"It's very fine, I dare say," said the old woman, for those who can get hold of it, but I have no understanding."

"Cannot you understand it?" asked Jane with disappointment.

"No, I never had any learning."

Jane looked down on the sacred words, and pondered what to say.

"I wish you could understand!" at last said Jane, looking up earnestly at the old woman's face; "if you could it would make you happy! Shall I read it over once again?"

"As you please," replied the old woman, "but I have no understanding."

Jane read a few verses again, then stopped, saying "Do you know who 'the Lamb' means?"

"No," answered the old woman.

"It means Jesus, the Son of God, because He died for us!" said Jane. Then Jane read on about the white robes, and stopped again and said, "Everybody in Heaven wears a white robe, because Jesus has washed them all white from their sins in His blood! I can teach you a prayer about that—it is a very short prayer out of the Bible—'Wash me, and I shall be whiter than snow.' Do say it after me, and then you will know it!"

The old woman tried; at last she seemed able to remember it a little:—and when Jane was gone, she still sat on her broken chair, saying over to herself, "Wash me whiter than snow! Wash me whiter than snow!"

It was simple teaching, and simple learning; but we must estimate the full meaning of the few words left in the aged woman's heart, before we can estimate the value of the lesson given and received. "Wash me!" there lay the assertion of her need of cleansing—a need only to be truly learned from the entrance of that Word that enlighteneth the eyes. "Whiter than snow!"—there lay the assurance that there was a power that could make clean,—make without spot the heart and life, that needed washing—unable to cleanse itself. When the Word of God, that gives at once the knowledge of sin and the only remedy, is once fixed within the heart, the nail is fastened in a sure place — though the Master of assemblies deign to work by the infant of days in fixing it there.

Jane's pence were now saved up by her eager, joyful hand of love, for her own old woman. First two lilac print aprons were bought and made, with a white one for Sundays. Mrs. Mansfield added a large handkerchief to pin outside the gown over the shoulders, which Jane hemmed: and when these were about to be taken, Mrs.

Mansfield said, "Suppose, if I can find a piece of black silk, I make her a little black bonnet?" Of course the thought of this was delightful, and Jane kept back her gifts till the bonnet was ready. The neatest old woman's bonnet was made; the silk put plain on a small close shape, and then Mrs. Mansfield made a plain net cap, with a net border, while Jane watched her mother's needle with eager interest. The bonnet and cap were put in a little blue bandbox; and then Mrs. Mansfield found a shawl of her own for the old woman; and so, richly-laden and overflowing with gladness, Jane set out, with her nurse and her brother to help, and the little ones to share the interest, on the way to her old woman's cottage. Tears started to the eyes of the poor old woman—tears of love and grateful feeling; and Jane saw the old woman at church—in her white apron, and neck-handkerchief and shawl, and her little black bonnet and white net cap. The hand of love had clothed her, the voice of love had warmed and cheered her; there were tones that make the heart's music now on Earth for her; and led by these, she went to hear of the love that these bore witness to — the love that passeth knowledge!"

Before the cold of winter had passed away, Jane discovered that her own old woman had stiff limbs from rheumatism; she told this, as

M. C.

she told everything, to her mother; and on Mrs. Mansfield's learning from Jane that the old woman's floor was damp, and without any covering, Mrs. Mansfield found up a variety of pieces of carpet, old and new, and showed Jane how to join them. With a pair of gloves on her hands, fine twine, and a short carpet-needle Jane sat on a low stool on the nursery floor and made her patchwork rug. It was kept a great secret, the old woman was to know nothing about it till it was done, and never could work have afforded a child more pleasure. She was to take the many-coloured rug, when finished, and lay it down herself; it would fill up all the space between the bed and the fire, just where the old woman sat, and light up with its variety of patterns and colours the dreary dwelling; the little window had long been cleaned, by the old woman's own hand, to let in more light for Jane to read; and Jane had secret thoughts of asking her mother if she might not make a little curtain for it; but the carpet-work fully engaged her spare time for the present; and sometimes her mother and sometimes her nurse gave her advice as to how best to arrange her various-shaped pieces. One day, while Jane was intent on her work in the middle of the nursery floor, the daughter of a neighbour and friend of her mother's knocked at the nursery-door, and on nurse saying, "Come in," she opened the door, saying, by way of excuse for her appearance there, "I found your mamma was out, and I got the servant just to let me run up, because I have no time to stay, and I want you to come to drink tea with us on Friday. I am to have a party. Mamma has bought me a new best frock of green silk, and I shall wear it then! What is your best frock?"

"I have no best frock," said Jane, "only one old stuff and one new stuff; and I wear white on Sundays in summer, and when I go out with mamma, if you mean that?"

"No, I wear white sometimes in summer; but how very odd you should not have a best frock! Shall you come in your stuff frock then?"

"I don't think mamma will let me come at all," said Jane, "I never go out to tea without mamma, unless it is with nurse into the country in summer-time."

"Well, but you will ask, will you not?"

"Yes, I will ask mamma," said Jane.

"What are you doing here?" said Jane's young visitor, looking down on the patchwork carpet, "sewing bits of carpet, I declare! what terrible hard work! I never have such work to do!"

"It is not hard," said Jane; "I like it very much, it's for a poor old woman who has nothing to lay on her floor, and her floor is damp!"

"O, well, I don't know any old woman; but if

I did, I think I should get my mamma to buy her a bit of carpet!"

"Mamma says," replied Jane, "that it is much better to give what we have made; and I know my old woman will like it a great deal the more for my having made it! And mamma says it will be much stronger and warmer than a new piece, because of all the joins I have made!"

"O yes, I dare say it will! but if you come and see me on Friday, I will show you my work; I am working a little boy and girl in worsted, sitting on a stool, and they have such rosy faces! I think I shall give it to mamma when I have finished it; but I don't know, because mamma says she is tired of the sight of it; but if I don't give it to mamma, I shall find some one else to give it to!"

When her young visitor was gone, Jane said to her nurse, "Do you think mamma would like it if I were to work some children sitting on a stool for her?"

"Nonsense!" said nurse, "your mamma sees enough of children sitting on stools, without your wasting your time in showing her. I have no patience with such folly; you had much better make carpets all your life for those who have none!"

"I never made anything for mamma!" said Jane.

"Well, you may be sure your mamma is best pleased when you are working for the Poor; but if you want to make something for her, I can tell you what would be a great deal better than children sitting on stools!"

"What, nurse?"

"Why, net her a purse! she uses one of those wove things, that look old before ever they look new? you might make her one that would look and wear well, and there would be some sense in that!"

"But I cannot do netting, nurse."

"O, I can soon teach you that! if you save up your pence for three weeks, you can buy a skein and begin. I have got a needle and pin."

"But will mamma know?"

"There is no need she should; if you like to be up these light mornings, you may work an hour before breakfast, by three weeks' time it may be a great deal warmer than now; but then you must save up all your money, because there will be the rings and the tassels as well as the silk."

The agreement was joyfully made. Now came the finishing of the patchwork-carpet; and Jane, with her nurse's help, carried it up to the old woman, and laid it down before her wondering eyes, and then looked around with delighted feeling at the change in the cottage, and the change in the dear old woman, since the day when first she entered it.

The purse could not be begun till the first threepence was saved up.

"You don't know why I save up my money now, mamma!" said Jane to her mother.

"No, indeed, I cannot tell, do you want a few of my pence to help yours a little, that I may know the sooner?"

"O, no, mamma, that would not do at all, it must be all my own money!" But while the child answered "No," she felt the confidence that would have helped her secret purpose without even asking to know it.

Jane could not quite forget her young visitor's remarks, so one day she said to her nurse, "Mamma never buys me a best frock!"

"No, nor does not need," replied nurse; "it's only those who don't look always as they should, and who want to look sometimes as they should not, who think about best dresses! Your mamma always keeps you neat, and fit to be seen according to your station, and so you have no more need to think about wanting a best frock than any lady in the land."

There was something so decided and satisfactory to Jane in her nurse's reply, that she thought no more upon the the subject, quite convinced that to be always neat was the only point of importance. But she could not so readily forget the worsted work; and though she was intent on her secret purse she still thought would it be very pleasant to do some work with coloured wools; she did not go to her young visitor's party, so she had not seen the work of which she had heard so much. "Mamma," said Jane, one day, "should you think that children sitting on a stool, would look pretty done in worsted work?"

"I do not know, unless I saw them," replied her mother, "but I do not generally admire such pieces of work; they take a great deal of time and attention, more, I think, than they are worth. Did you wish to try some worsted work?"

"Yes, mamma, I should like it very much, only nurse said it was nonsense to work children sitting on a stool, and I don't know what else could be done!"

"A great many things can be done! I think the best would be, to work your father a pair of worsted slippers, to put on when he comes in from the shop; nurse would not think that nonsense."

"O, yes, I should like that a great deal the best. May I do that, mamma?"

"Yes, you shall go to a shop with me and choose them for yourself."

And so the child found full employment now, in her early work for her mother, and her later work for her father—all through the spring's bright weeks; and then the joy of presenting her gifts, and seeing the lasting pleasure with which they were used—the smile of remembrance that fell on her glad eyes when the purse was drawn out sometimes, or the slippers put on. And thus, within and without her home, every pure and hallowed sympathy was strengthened in her young life by natural and easy exercise.

VIII.

The Little Comforter.

"The world's a room of sickness, where each heart
Knows it's own anguish and unrest;
The truest wisdom there, and noblest art,
Is his, who skills of comfort best."

In the following Spring an invitation came for Rose, from her mother's only brother, a farmer on a large grass farm in Derbyshire; it was a long journey for Rose to take, and her father was very unwilling to lose his little comforter from his home; Rose also did not like the thought of another visit to unknown relations, but her mother was resolved—Mrs. Smith said that her brother would have good reason to be offended, as Rose had been allowed to visit her other uncle, if his invitation was refused; so the engagement was made, and Rose was to meet her uncle in London, to which place he expected to travel up in about three weeks' time; and as in those days it was not thought worth while for children to take a long journey for a short period, it was settled that Rose was to spend three months beneath her Derbyshire uncle's roof.

When Molly, the maid at the farm, found that Rose was to leave for another long visit, her patient endurance gave way to despair, and after nine years' faithful service she told her mistress that she must leave her place—unable to bear the prospect of her mistress's trying temper without Rose to soften it. Things were not improved in the house by Molly's giving warning; Mrs. Smith really valued her, and was very sorry to lose her; but the pride of heart which made Mrs. Smith's temper so trying to all, would not now suffer her to express any regret—she only showed resentment at what she called Molly's ingratitude; and Rose left her home with a sorrowful heart.

When the time for Molly's departure arrived, she came to take leave of her mistress in tears—little Tim had run off crying, to hide himself in the stable—and Molly gathered courage and said, "I am sure, ma'am, I never would have left your place for another, if I might have reckoned on a pleasant word sometimes; but I don't think, since master Joe and the horse went away, you have given me so much as one—and I'm sure that their going was none of my doing; and I can't stand it, ma'am, and I don't see who is to stand it!" There still were moments when Mrs. Smith's pride had almost more than enough to do in keeping down and hiding up the buried feeling of her heart; and now when her faithful, her really valued servant, stood before her and confessed that her mistress could have bound her to her service by a pleasant word; when that servant was really departing, Mrs. Smith found the only disguise for her feeling would be silence; she held out Molly's wages without looking at her, and then turned another way; while poor Molly, quite overcome, left the farm for her mother's distant village, with a feeling of unreturned affection and heart-breaking distress.

There was one person — and only one — with whom Mrs. Smith had to do, to whom she had never spoken a harsh word; it was not Rose, it was not little Tim, it was not her favourite William; no, it was the orphan child, Mercy Jones. It was true, the orphan's grandmother, widow Jones, had always stood as high as possible in Mrs. Smith's regard; Jem also, Mercy's uncle, Mrs. Smith considered worth all the other men and boys on the farm put together, because she said, "If you make him understand what is to be done, you may give up the worry yourself!" But it was not her grandmother and her uncle's good qualities that procured such favour for Mercy; Mrs. Smith was a strict examiner of each individual with whom she had to do, and nothing but personal integrity could ever win her regard. Mercy was a tall, delicate-looking, gentle child, with a thoughtful heart, a willing mind, and a ready skill, that far more than compensated for her lack of strength; and now that for the first time in nine years the farm was left without a maid, widow Jones and Mercy both came in to help. It might have been supposed that these two helpers would prove equal to Molly's former service, and so they might have been, but for Mrs. Smith's apprehensions on Mercy's behalf: "Here, give that to me, girl," she would continually say, taking the work from Mercy's hands, and finishing it up with equal energy and seven-fold power; then, adding kindly, "It's not, as I say, because you have not the notion, but because you have not the strength!" While to her husband Mrs. Smith was constantly declaring, "Slave as I may, I am sure that girl will be overdone! she is too willing, and the work's beyond her, and an orphan as she is—I wish enough I could meet with some one I should not always be afraid to put upon!" Many girls came and offered themselves, but Mrs. Smith declared that there was not so much as one among them who had any right to the name of a servant; she could tell that without any need of a trial! All this time, while vexing over Mercy's toil, overworking her own strength, and objecting to every girl who came before her, Mrs. Smith never named the absent Molly; in all the vexatious trouble she daily made for herself, she cast no fresh censure on Molly, and could Molly have seen her mistress's real feeling, the probability would have been her instant return to offer her services again; but pride lay between Mrs. Smith's heart and her lips, and kept her continually back from the confessions that would have led to peace in her family, instead of strife and debate.

All through the years of which we have been speaking, Patience had lived on in her place of service with the family of Mr. Mansfield's foreman; but her master and mistress had for some time felt that the increasing expenses of their growing family were putting a servant beyond their means: and a still stronger reason for doing without one lay in the good sense of these excellent parents, who felt that the best way of teaching their children diligence and method in accomplishing work, would be to bring them up to get well through all that their own home required. But how to send Patience away was the painful part; and month after month, then week after week, her dismissal was delayed, till at last the foreman's wife said, "Well, I cannot help it, she has worked like a child for me, and you must tell her, for I can't; you hired her, she knows, and so it will come natural to her!" It was very seldom that the good woman's resolution failed her, but now it did; and her husband's mild firmness came in to the rescue of their home principles. He told Patience, quietly and decidedly, that he felt the time had come when his girls must do all the work of the house; that both he and his wife valued her faithful services, and still more the example she had set their children; he said she had earned what was better than any wages—the lasting regard of those she had served! and he told her to come to his house, as a home always open to her, while she maintained the same character she had earned in his family. The colour left the cheek of Patience, and she could not speak; her master added kindly, that they should not think of parting with her till she met with a comfortable place, therefore she need feel no anxiety on that subject, and then left her. When Patience returned to her mistress and the children, her tears broke forth, her good mistress cried also, and the children cried; but her mistress making an effort said cheerfully, "Come, child, its not for you to fret, you have done your duty here, and your reward will follow; you are only going to make more friends, and not to lose those you leave behind; so cheer up, and be as busy as you can; that's the best cure for low spirits of most kinds!" So Patience tried, but the spring of her work was gone, she worked well as before, but it was the work of habit and principle, not the energy of life; and often through her heart a faintness passed as she felt the home was hers no longer; she must wander out again into the world her childhood found so rough! and thoughts of her early life, and of her first place of service, came back with a sinking weight on her spirit.

Having spoken to Patience, her master now named the subject to his employer, Mr. Mansfield, and Mr. Mansfield promised to name it to some of his best customers; among the first of these, on the next day, being market-day, was farmer Smith.

"It's no use to ask you, Mr. Smith, whether you want a servant-girl, for yours knows the value of her place, it seems, too well to leave it!"

"Ah, she is gone at last!" replied farmer Smith, gravely. "Yes, hers was nine years of honest service; she earned her wages fairly enough, but she is gone at last!"

"Well, then, I can find you just such another! my foreman here, like a wise man, is giving up servant-keeping; and he wants a place, he says, for one of the best girls who ever called herself a servant."

At this the foreman came forward and talked with farmer Smith, and Mr. Mansfield waited on his other customers.

Now Mrs. Smith had often said that she would rather by far teach a girl farm-work and farm-ways from the beginning, than have one who thought herself clever at everything! So farmer Smith went home, thinking he had met with the very girl most likely to satisfy his wife; but Mrs. Smith was not in a mood to be satisfied with any thing or anybody, and only replied to farmer Smith's pleasant description: "And what's the use of a girl that never stirred from the town, and knows only town ways, out here in the country?"

"Why, a good servant is a good servant!" replied Mr. Smith; "and as for our ways, why, she can learn the country ways I suppose as well as she learned the town ways—if she has a mind to them!"

"But it is not in the least likely she would have a mind to them; girls who have been used to the town never settle in country places like this; she had a thousand times better stay where she is!" said Mrs. Smith.

Farmer Smith found it was hopeless to urge the point, so he dropped the subject. On the next market-day he made one more attempt, asking Mrs. Smith if she would not like to go in and just see the girl? but Mrs. Smith replied that she could judge about it quite as well without having to go seven miles to come to an opinion! so farmer Smith took his drive to the town alone. He called at Mr. Mansfield's shop, and requested the foreman to wait one week longer for his answer, which he readily consented to do, as he thought the place must be a good one where the last servant had remained nine years; farmer Smith's character also stood very high; and Patience was quite willing to go. "Moreover," the foreman added, "my opinion is, that the girl will settle all the better a little distance from my wife and children, of whom she is wonderfully fond!" So farmer Smith, very anxious to secure a good girl for his wife and home, waited for the forlorn hope of Mrs. Smith's change of feeling by another market-day.

The week passed by: every girl who applied for the place was pronounced by Mrs. Smith to be as unfit as could be, and the last person she would think of engaging with! while she still vexed at having no servant to do the work, and protested that Mercy would be ill with overdoing—but farmer Smith heard it all in perfect silence. The next market-day arrived, but farmer Smith asked no questions; he prepared as usual for market; when, just as with hat and whip he was leaving the house, Mrs. Smith followed him and said, "There is not the least use in the world in my going all that way after a girl that is not likely to come, or to stay if she did come; but if she has a mind to come after the place herself, why, that's another thing."

"When would you like her to come then?" inquired farmer Smith, "supposing she is willing?"

"Why, the sooner the better! I am sure I am in a fidget about that child Mercy, every day of my life; it's a wonder that she is not overset already, and I also, with the work of such a place as this is!"

Farmer Smith stepped quietly into his gig and drove off. In the evening he returned with Patience seated beside him.

"What have you been after now?" exclaimed Mrs. Smith, in dismay, calling farmer Smith aside privately; "that's just the way with you, never giving one time to turn round, you think a thing is no sooner said than it can be done! I never meant the girl to come for good till I had seen her!"

"Well, wife," replied farmer Smith quietly, "there is no harm done, the girl could not make her way out here alone; if you don't fancy her, Jem can drive her back in the light cart after tea —or you can keep her a week on trial, both her mistress and the girl were willing either way."

Hearing this, Mrs. Smith was somewhat pacified, and she went out to receive Patience who stood waiting at the door. There stood Patience, a stout strongly-built young woman, with a fresh colour and a pleasant face, her dress neatness itself. When she saw her expected mistress, Patience made a low curtsey, such as she had been used to make in her school days in the town, and she stood silently before Mrs. Smith. Now Mrs. Smith was not naturally without kindness of heart; it was pride and selfishness which she had suffered to grow within her unrestrained, that blinded her to the feelings of others; but when she saw a stranger girl before her, one of whom she heard so good a character, her natural kindness rose unimpeded, she received her with a welcome, and said as she had come so far, and had brought her things with her, she had at all events better stay the week.

Patience rose the next morning almost at break of day, she opened her little window and wondered at the fragrance of the air; she looked over the land, and while she sighed for the sleeping children far away, and the cheerful call of her mistress's kind, quick tone that could not reach her now—while she sighed for these, she felt that she could love those pleasant fields better far than the town, and that if she could but bring her master's family to her, she should never wish for the town again: but then the feeling of a stranger in a strange place came over her, and she could only turn from the window to commit herself in prayer to Him who is the stranger's God. As soon as Patience heard her mistress moving, she left the room, and, greatly to the surprise of Mrs. Smith, her new maid stood before her at five o'clock in the morning, in her neat gown of dark blue with short sleeves, and a stout apron—as fit for farm-house work as for any other. There was about Patience a quietness of look and manner that made a striking contrast with her active figure and step, quick without haste, and quiet without dulness; it might be that the exterior of her early sorrow had never been quite effaced, but left its gentle shade upon her life's after vigour and brightness. There was also a propriety of manner about Patience, that could not fail to produce a pleasing impression; and a readiness of attention, and willingness of movement, that made it no effort to tell her to do anything—while her thoughtful care more frequently prevented the need of her being told. Mrs. Smith's quick eye soon read these qualifications; and the consequence was, she instantly made up her mind that Patience would consider herself too good for the place, and would be certain not to stay; but still as she felt her deserving of attention, she put her in the way of farm-house work, giving her daily instruction in milking and other peculiarities of the diary. Patience was very grave, for her heart was still in her last place, she was always finding herself back again in thought with those she had left; and Mrs. Smith failed not to set this down as discontent. "But, surely," said farmer Smith, "the girl does everything in as pleasant a way as can be done, and what would you have more?"

"Oh, that's only by way of keeping up her character!" replied Mrs. Smith, "you will see she will never stay a day beyond her week; I am sure she will never come down to the place, her manners are above it!"

Mrs. Smith did not know that she had one beneath her roof who had been humbled in sorrow's bitter school; one whose heart no money could win, but which affection's power or feeling's claim could bind to any service; so she made up her mind that Patience would consider herself above the place and go; and she said it was very hard to have nothing before her but teaching the same things over and over again to a dozen girls one after another, for she was sure the place would never suit this girl, and it was not likely she would find a girl in a hurry that would suit her! Farmer Smith heard in silence.

The end of the week came; Patience said nothing, so Mrs. Smith expressed her opinion in a few words.

"Well, girl, you have done full as well as any one might expect; but of course the place is not one to suit you, any one can see that; so I can only wish you a better! We will make out a way to get you back to your friends." Patience looked up in surprise, and the colour deepened in her cheeks; "I have no wish to leave the place, ma'am," she replied, "if I could suit you; I am not likely to find a better."

Mrs. Smith was now more surprised than Patience had been, and not altogether pleased at finding herself mistaken; for Mrs. Smith always felt a secret satisfaction in seeing her predictions fulfilled, even though she considered the events to be evil. Happily Patience had said that she did not think herself likely to find a better place, and this single expression of feeling from a heart in which pride had no indulgence, went far to relieve the involuntary annoyance Mrs. Smith felt at finding her own impression a wrong one. So Patience stayed.

But from the day on which Mrs. Smith looked upon Patience as really her servant, she began her usual tone of harsh authority. Patience was neither slow to learn, nor frequent in forgetting; but the dread of her mistress's voice made her painfully anxious about every possible thing that could be expected of her; and the dull heavy look of her childhood began to steal over and shadow the pleasant expression of her face. She would sometimes watch little Tim in the farm-yard by the side of his father, or talking with Jem, and she would think that child seemed the only one that she could love; but he was seldom within, always running away as soon as possible from his mother's harsh voice; he was a favourite with all the labourers, and they would do anything to please him; but Jem was his chief friend; from the time that William had left, he had taken to Jem—as if he considered him to be most like his lost brother, and no one could so easily wake the clear tones of his merry laugh as honest Jem: he would ride on his shoulders, wander down to find him with the sheep, share his homely food, and now that Rose was away, he would get to him whenever he could. Poor Patience used to watch the child, and wish that he would turn to her as he did to Jem; but Molly was still fresh in the memory of little Tim, and he scarcely looked at Patience. So Patience felt more and more desolate, while closer round her heart pressed the warm memories of the home she had left.

While things were in this state, Jem, who had been sent on an errand to the town, came into the back-kitchen to have some food on his return; it was evening, and Patience was sitting there alone. Jem had often observed her disconsolate look, and it hurt his kind and honest heart to see so little comfort for her; and now as he sat on the back-kitchen bench cutting his bread and meat with his great pocket-knife, he ventured a remark: "Living out here in the country, I take it, doesn't suit you like down there in the town?"

"No, it's very different!" replied Patience; and there was silence again.

"You seem hard done up in your thoughts," again observed Jem; "I hope you haven't happened with any misfortune!"

"No, not exactly that," Patience slowly replied; and then, encouraged by Jem's friendly tone, and not less by the expression of his honest face, which she had seen most days since she had been at the farm, she went on to say, "I was thinking how little wages I could do with! I think I could do with less than my last mistress would have liked to offer me; only then I remembered there's the food—and one must eat if one's to live!"

Jem had no skill in arithmetic, and could not render much aid in such a calculation; but he had a far quicker estimate, perhaps, than many an arithmetician, of the heart's joys and sorrows, and he came in with his friendly aid at the root of the matter. "Are you after a change then?" he asked.

"Well," replied Patience, "I was thinking if I could get back anyhow where I came from; I would rather live there on dry bread, than here, where nobody has a care for one, on any wages!"

"But," answered Jem, "they said you could not hold the place, because the family gave up servant-keeping?"

"So they did," said Patience, "and I'm afraid they would not take me back if I could go without wages; only I can't help thinking about it!"

"Well, now," said Jem, "take my advice; you will never do yourself or others a straw's worth of good, thinking on what cannot be; and don't be downhearted here; mistress is hasty I know, but I have served her from a child, and if once you get right with her, you will never have a trouble from her again. She is always for thinking every one will go wrong till she finds they go no way but right; once let her get persuaded of that, and she would not believe the whole world if they stood out against you! I know it's hard in the coming, and she has been put out of late more than common one way or another; and the last maid could not put up with it, nor wait for things to work round again, so she left; but only you keep right on as you have begun, and you will be sure to find things mend in good time!"

This conversation was the first encouragement poor Patience had had; it eased her spirit also to have been able to speak on the subject, and for a time she went more cheerfully on. But the same harsh tone, the same cold short manner, met her every effort, and after a while she lost heart again, and began to think she must give up, and try to find some other place. But where could she turn? She had no opportunity, so far from the town, of making inquiry; and she was ashamed to write to her mistress, and say she could not stay in the place she had been so glad to secure for her. She was sitting at her needle on the low chair in the back-kitchen, and as she thought on these things her tears fell on her work. Little Tim had come, unperceived by her, to the back-door, and as he stood there looking in, he saw Patience crying. The sight touched his heart, for little Tim was no

PATIENCE AND LITTLE TIM.

stranger to tears, especially since Rose had been away; so he came up to Patience, and said in his kindest little voice, "What for you kie?"

"Because no one here loves me!" said Patience.

"I will love you!" said little Tim, putting his hand upon her cheek, and then, when Patience still cried, slipping his arm around her neck, he said again, "I will love you very much, don't kie any more!"

Patience clasped her arms round the child, and laid her head one moment on his little shoulder, as he stood beside her, and sobbed; then looking up, she made an effort and wiped away her tears, and said, "If you love me, then I will not cry!" From that time little Tim seemed to feel that it depended upon him to keep Patience from crying; he would often come and look at her from the back-kitchen door, and when she was alone would stay beside her and talk to her; and the heart of poor Patience grew content in her place — because of the love and care of that one little ministering child.

Rose had now been more than two months away, and they had proved happy months for her. Her uncle met her in London—a grave and silent person, of whom Rose felt afraid; but her aunt's kind face, and her cousins' warm greeting, soon made her at home among them. She found every one of them full of occupation; but each one seemed ready for her, and always able to find her a help and comfort. She helped her cousins tend their poultry, and make the summer preserves—learning many things unknown in her home. She helped them in their garden, where she learned from them to bud roses, prune trees, and as the summer advanced, to distil rose-leaves and herbs. She helped them in their work—she learned to cut out and make by herself garments for the poor; and often while she worked with them, one read aloud, and Rose learned more of general knowledge in that visit, than in all her young life before. Here she heard histories of Missions, all new to her; and read of other countries also new and strange to her. She sat by her cousins while they taught the village children in the school, till at last they made her take a little class of her own; this gave new interest and delight to Rose, and she thought it would be as hard to leave the little children of her class as it would to leave anything. She wondered how she could have lived so long without knowing and loving relations so dear to her now! but the distance had been great between them. Still Rose often thought of her home, and longed to see it again, though she did not like to think of leaving her aunt and cousins far away. But when the harvest-time came, and Rose was expecting to return, a letter arrived to say that little Tim was ill with a dangerous fever, and the letter asked that Rose might still remain at her uncle's house, for fear of her taking the fever if she returned. This was unexpected sorrow for Rose — little Tim, whom she loved so much, dangerously ill, and she could not nurse, or comfort, or see him! Poor Rose was overwhelmed with grief, but she had those around her now who knew how to comfort; they loved her more tenderly in her sorrow than they had done before, and they reminded her to whom to look—even to the Saviour who can comfort any heart that turns to Him.

Little Tim lay in his cot at home, and the doctor said that his life was in danger. Now a real trial was come to Mrs. Smith at last; she had long been making troubles for herself and others, but trouble was come now, and she felt it was; and all that before she had made so much of was forgotten. Day and night she watched by the cot of little Tim; he did not like to lie in her arms when restless—he seemed uneasy there, and cried for Rose when his mother took him; so, weeping, she would lay him back upon his pillow, and sit long hours and watch beside him. As she sat there, a sense of the past came over her—a sense of years of harshness and ill-temper; of peace destroyed by her, and sorrow made for others; she thought, too, of how the child had always seemed glad to slip away from her, as if uneasy in her presence; and she looked down on his burning cheek and felt as if it would kill her to see him die. Patience too would watch beside the cot while widow Jones did her work below—and it seemed to ease the heavy grief of Mrs. Smith to have her there. The men were constantly inquiring for the child, and Jem was always waiting about the house, when possible, helping his mother do the work, and asking of all who came from the room how the child seemed now?

Mrs. Smith was leaning over the cot, and Patience kneeling beside it, when little Tim called, "Rose! Rose! Come to Tim! Come now!"

"What do you want, my darling?" said Mrs. Smith, "I will do it for you!" "I want to puay," said little Tim, "and Rose can teach me, I forget it now!" Mrs. Smith was silent.

"Mother, can you puay?" asked little Tim. Mrs. Smith hid her face and wept, she felt she could not pray; she had never taught her child, and she could not teach him now, she could think of nothing!

"Can you puay, Patens?" asked little Tim, in his anxiety. "Yes, dear, I do pray for you."

"Oh then you can teach it to me! I forget it all now!" said little Tim, and he joined his hands together in act of prayer.

Patience repeated the prayer she had taught to little Esther in her last place, and Tim, quite satisfied, repeated it after her.

"Can you say my texes too?" asked little Tim.

Patience made a guess, and said, "Suffer the little children to come unto Me, and forbid them not, for of such is the kingdom of Heaven," it proved quite right, and little Tim added, "I can say my other, 'Speak, Lord, for thy servant heareth.'"

"Now I can say my hymn," said little Tim, "that Rose did teach me!" and looking up with folded hands he repeated in his broken utterance—

"Lord, look upon a little child,
By nature sinful, rude, and wild;
O put Thy gracious hands on me,
And make me what I ought to be.

"Make me Thy child—a child of God,
Washed in my Saviour's precious blood;
And my whole heart from sin set free,
A little vessel full of Thee.

"A star of early dawn and bright,
Shining within Thy sacred light;
A beam of grace to all around;
A little spot of hallowed ground.

"Lord Jesus, take me to Thy breast,
And bless me that I may be blest;
Both when I wake, and when I sleep,
Thy little lamb in safety keep."

And then, quite satisfied, he said, "Mother, don't kie any more—Patens can teach it me all!" and turning his cheek on his pillow, he fell peacefully asleep

Day and night Mrs. Smith repeated to herself, and tried to keep in her memory continually, the prayer that Patience had said for little Tim, in the hope that he would ask her again to teach him—but he never appealed to his mother any more; when he woke from sleep, if he had his senses, his first look was for Patience, and with folded hands he waited for her to teach him "how to pray!"

"Does it hurt you very much, dear?" asked Patience, as she helped Mrs. Smith to dress a blister on the child's head. "No, nothing hurts me now!" said little Tim. And he soon after drew his last breath, and died.

It was grief for all: but the mother's heart was broken up; she took to her bed, the fever that had taken little Tim from Earth came upon her, and her mind wandered in sorrowful delirium. Patience was her devoted nurse; while widow Jones sometimes gave Patience a little rest from the sick-room, or helped her in it, and at other times did what she could of the work below, with Jem to aid.

"I see it now!" said Mrs. Smith, when for a short time her senses returned, "I see it all now, it is right I should be left to die! I turned from our young Minister who would have taught me how to live; and now death is come, and I see plain enough that I am not ready to meet it!"

"Don't you think the Minister would come, if he was asked?" said Patience, to widow Jones.

"What's the use of it?" asked widow Jones, "she is scarcely a moment reasonable, and she has been so set against him, it might be too much for her now!"

Widow Jones had seen their aged Minister sent for to the dying; but he had never unlocked the exhaustless treasury of the love of God in Jesus Christ for his own heart—therefore he knew not how to dispense its balm of Life, its soothing peace to others: widow Jones had never seen the servant of the most High God, the faithful Minister of the truth as it is in Jesus, draw near in his Master's name to the dying bed where hope was not—this she had never seen, and so knowing only what she had seen, she only replied, "What's the use?"

But Patience was not to be so easily satisfied; she waited awhile, and then she went to her master: "My poor mistress keeps lamenting so," she said, "to think how she turned from the Minister! Don't you think he would come to see her if you asked him, sir?"

Farmer Smith stood silent, "It's a hard case!" he replied, "I am sure I don't know; I have been ashamed to meet him for ever so long now, and it's more than a year since he has been into the house—your poor mistress was so set against him; and now such a fever as it is,—and her senses gone—I don't know that I dare to ask it!"

"May I go, sir, and just tell him the state my poor mistress is in, and hear if he would please to come?"

"But," said farmer Smith, "it might overset her, so bad as she is, and then if she were worse, I should have to answer for it—I dare not engage with it!"

So Patience returned to the sick chamber. The sun was setting in the autumnal evening, she sat down by the window and looked into the glowing sky, and thought of little Tim—the thought was sad, yet full of peace. Lost in the feeling, she watched the sun's decline behind the purple clouds; then looking down below again, she saw a distant figure crossing the pasture in the valley; it was the Curate! could he indeed be coming to the farm? or would he take the road that led to the cottages by the wood? Patience watched, breathless between hope and fear! He crossed the farm-stile, he turned to the bridge over the brook, and then began to ascend the green slope—he was coming indeed! Patience ran down, farmer Smith was still within; he hastened out to meet his visitor, and Patience returned to see that all was in readiness above.

"I am grieved to hear of your heavy trials," said the Curate, as he entered the house with farmer Smith. "I was absent at the death of your child, and only now heard on my return, of the illness of your wife. I thought she might be willing to see me; but if not, I hope I may be permitted to speak a word of comfort to you."

"I am sure, sir, it is more than I could have expected!" said farmer Smith, hardly able to speak from overburdened feeling.

"It is a dark and cloudy day for you!" said the Curate. "A storm has burst upon you! but you remember how after the storm the bow is set in the cloud for all who will look above to the hand that smites them—the storm has come, and now we must look up, and wait and watch in prayer and faith, for the rainbow of promise and comfort! Will your wife be able and willing to see me?"

Mr. Smith went to the sick room, and returned, saying, "She is not sensible, sir, and I am afraid it is but putting you into danger."

"Oh, I am not afraid of that!" replied the Curate,—"if you are willing I should go; we may pray for her, and more may be known by her than you think."

"Well, then, sir, if you please!" said farmer Smith. And the feet of the publisher of peace, the bringer of good tidings, entered the chamber of sickness and sorrow. He stood a moment by the bed and looked upon the poor unconscious sufferer, then saying, "Let us pray," he knelt down beside the bed, while farmer Smith and Patience knelt also.

"O God of the spirits of all flesh, Thou who art a just God, and yet a Saviour, hear us, we beseech Thee, in the prayer which we offer up through Thy Son Jesus Christ, for the body and soul of this sick woman. In Thy most merciful Hands are the issues of life and death: O suffer not the king of terrors to destroy, but raise her up, we beseech Thee, that she may live in Thy sight. O spare her, most merciful Lord, now that Thou hast dug with Thy chastening Hand to her roots; O spare her, we pray Thee, yet another year, to see if she may not now bear fruit to Thy honour and praise and glory! Open Thou her ear, good Lord, to hear Thy still small voice in this hour of tribulation: open Thou her eyes, to behold the Lamb of God who taketh away all sin: open Thou her heart, to receive Him whom Thou hast sent to seek and to save that which was lost. As Thou hast ploughed up her soul with affliction, O cast in the precious seed of Thy word, and so water it with Thy grace and nourish it with Thy blessing, that it may bring forth fruit unto life eternal. And cause, we beseech Thee, the doctrine of Thy grace and the word of Thy lips to distil as the dew at this time upon the parched spirit of this poor sufferer, that she may know the power of its Heavenly refreshment. We ask all for His sake whose precious blood cleanseth from all sin, and whose Spirit quickeneth the dead, even Jesus Christ our Lord. Amen."

Then, sitting down beside the bed, the Minister repeated softly and slowly, "Come unto me all ye that labour and are heavy laden, and I will give you rest." "Come now, and let us reason together, saith the Lord; though your sins be as scarlet, they shall be as white as snow; though they be red like crimson, they shall be as wool." "The blood of Jesus Christ cleanseth from all sin." "Look unto Me, and be ye saved, all the ends of the earth; for I am God, and there is none else." "Ask, and it shall be given you; seek, and ye shall find; knock, and it shall be opened unto you; for every one that asketh, receiveth; and he that seeketh, findeth; and to him that knocketh it shall be opened." The words, the tone of peace, seemed to soothe the sufferer—she lay still and composed. The Minister said fervently, "The Lord bless thee and keep thee; the Lord make His face to shine upon thee, and be gracious unto thee; the Lord lift up the light of His countenance upon thee, and give thee peace!" And then he left the room.

The Curate talked long with farmer Smith below,

who found, to his surprise, that there was no resentment at the conduct poor Mrs. Smith had shown towards him; he only spoke the words and breathed the spirit of sympathy, and counsel, and comfort. Oh, what a weight was lifted that evening from the heart of farmer Smith! The opposition expressed and shown in his home, had kept him back from venturing to speak to the Curate; but now he had been seated with him in his own parlour without fear, and there had been able to utter the long pent-up and hidden feelings of his heart. How the father thought of his little Rose, as he returned with thankfulness and peace to his kitchen!

"Patience, child, is it you?" said Mrs. Smith that evening, when the light of day had faded, and the candle was lit. "Patience, child, is it you? I hardly seem to know where I am, and yet I think I am better! I have had such a Heavenly dream—I thought I was carried, all so bad as I am, in my bed to the church, and there I saw the new Minister again! Oh, how it seemed to give me hope, for I thought I had turned away from him, and now I should never be suffered to see him any more! I thought he stood up, but he seemed to speak only to me, and to look down at none but me, and he preached about "rest!" and it seemed as if he came with the message for me, straight from the God above; and then I thought I looked round for little Tim to hear the sweet words too, but he was not there, and then I remembered he was gone! but still it did not seem to strike me down as the thought of him did before, for I seemeed to know that he was gone to that "rest" that the Minister was preaching about. Oh, how it did ease me to hear our new Minister again! Patience, child, do you think I shall ever be able to get to the church any more, before I am carried to my grave?"

"O yes, dear mistress, I do think you will live, by God's mercy; and that was not all a dream you had, it was part true, for the Minister has been here to see you!"

"The Rector?"

"No, the Curate himself! and oh, I feel sure since he came and prayed for your life, and your pardon, and peace, that God will give it!"

"What! our Curate been here to see me!"

"Yes, and he stood up by the bed, and he said those words, 'Come unto me, all ye that labour and are heavy laden, and I will give you rest!'"

"Why, those are the very words I seemed to hear him preach upon! Who could have thought it! Do you think he will come again?"

"Yes, I am sure he will," replied Patience; "and he will find you better when he does!"

The next day the Curate called again. Mrs. Smith had been saved all anxiety of expectation—

not thinking he would come so soon; she was much overcome at seeing him, saying to him, "Oh, sir, I thought I should never have seen you again!"

"My Master has sent me to comfort all who mourn," said the Minister, "and I hope by His grace to be able to comfort you!"

"Oh, sir, I don't know, but I fear not, I fear my comfort is dead, and I dying myself!"

"The Lord my God," said the Minister, "is one who quickeneth the dead! He can not only restore you, but comfort you also!"

"Ah, sir, I fear you don't know how bad I have been! I was set against your preaching from the first, because you said there was but one way for all, and you invited the worst of sinners to come and try that way, and it hurt my pride—I thought they were not fit to be put so along with me! but now I have seen that I am not fit to be put with them, for I am the worst of all!"

"I have then a message for you," said the Minister, "you have often heard it before, but now that God is chastening and teaching you, you will be able to understand its meaning, and I trust to receive its comfort. 'If we say that we have no sin, we deceive ourselves, and the truth is not in us. If we confess our sins, God is faithful and just to forgive us our sins, and to cleanse us from all unrighteousness.' You see then there is forgiveness for you—pardon and peace with God, through Jesus Christ our Lord, if confessing your sins unto God, you look to the Saviour, whom God has set forth to be a propitiation for sin."

Mrs. Smith listened to the words, and that truth which before had been so bitter was now sweet to her hungry soul. The visits of the minister were her greatest comfort. Till at last from that sick-bed, the tones of hope, and peace, and praise, were heard: and the always pleasant but now softened smile of Mrs. Smith would fall on those who watched beside her; and on Patience it fell with something of a mother's feeling.

The evening hearth shone bright when Mrs. Smith first came down to tea. Samson and Ted had done their best to make all things cheerful and full of comfort. Widow Jones had put away into the parlour Tim's little chair—but the mother's eye fell upon its vacant place. It was a long sad lesson that mother's heart had still to learn; but, sweetened by Heavenly mercy, and soothed by Heavenly peace, the longest lesson will only the more establish the heart, and root it the deeper in faith, hope, and love.

The autumn passed away, but fear of infection still made the anxious mother keep Rose from home. At last all danger was considered over, and the day was fixed for Rose to return; and her two brothers, William and Joe, were to join her in London, and return with her. What a day of expectation was that! Jem drove the horse in the gig to the next village inn, where the coach always stopped; then leaving it there, he walked back, and the two brothers, with Rose in the gig between them, drove home together. Far over the now empty fields gleamed the light from the farm-window, of the blazing logs heaped up by Ted upon the fire; the mother in her gown of black, sat in her chair beside it; the tea was prepared, and the pile of buttered toast, which Samson made in Rose's absence. Patience had an extra baking, with Widow Jones to help, and all her skill could do was added to the prepared reception. Patience had never seen Rose as yet, and her heart trembled at thought of the one for whom the dying child had called, returning to the home where he was not! But in they came, Rose first. "Mother! oh, mother!" said the child, and her mother held her, long-pressed in her close embrace—as if fearing that she too might pass away from her sight like little Tim! Then in came William and Joe, with their tender and gentle greeting; and with softened feeling on every face, and deeper love in every heart, the circle, from which one had been taken, drew round to their evening meal.

IX.

The Young Squire's Return.

Enthroned upon a hill of light,
  A heavenly minstrel sings;
And sounds unutterably bright,
  Spring from the golden strings.
Who would have thought so fair a form
Once bent beneath an earthly storm.

THE winter passed peacefully away at the farm. There was a hush about the place—a shadow evidently hung above it, the former active bustle of the house went on more quietly; but it was a stillness that told of greater depth, a shade beneath which the best feelings of the heart strengthened and grew. The look of anxiety which used so often to cross the young and blooming face of Rose, as she feared in time past, her mother's hasty feeling at every fresh proposal or event, had passed away; yet was her brightness blended with a quietness, that told the sense of something gone—which steadied the light spirits of her happy youth; steadied but did not sadden—for she shared the happiness of little Tim; and she often sung aloud the first verse of one of Mercy's hymns—

"There is beyond the sky
A Heaven of joy and love:
And holy children when they die,
Go to that world above!"

And though her mother never noticed it in words, yet did she often listen to the low tones as Rose sang on to herself; listened in fear lest the sweet sounds should cease; but happily Rose acquired the habit, till she would begin and go on almost unconsciously to herself. Sunday was now a day of rest indeed; a day made holy and a delight by the glad tidings of great joy, preached every Sabbath in the village church.

Patience had again found a home, and the heart of her mistress cherished for her a deeper feeling than any that Patience had known in service before. With Rose it was always pleasant to work, or to speak; and when Patience discovered the mutual friendship existing between Rose and a variety of the living creatures upon the farm, Patience took pattern, and trained her cows to an intelligence that seemed to give promise of rivalling, in time, the very horses themselves!

In the following summer, to the delight of Rose, her Derbyshire uncle and aunt and two of her cousins came down, at Mrs. Smith's earnest request, to make a visit at the farm. Mrs. Smith's brother soon returned to his home, on account of his business; but he left his wife and daughters, who made a stay of six weeks—to the comfort and profit of Mrs. Smith, the satisfaction and pleasure of farmer Smith, and the ceaseless enjoyment of Rose. This intercourse tended to raise and enlarge Mrs. Smith's already softened and rightly-directed feeling. And six weeks of so much peaceful enjoyment had never been known before within the farm.

William and Joe obtained an early holiday this year, and to their father's comfort and the pleasure of all, they came down for the last fortnight of the harvest-time. How merrily did Rose prepare the harvest-cakes the last baking before their return, obtaining from her mother's pleased and willing hand a larger supply of plums—because Will and Joe would be among those to be fed with the harvest-cakes! And though it was four years since William had held a sickle, the reapers declared that Master William might stand king of them, for all he had been up in London so long! But it was only a fortnight—and the time drew to its close. The father had felt again the comfort of his eldest son at his side in the anxiety and joy of harvest, and his spirits sank at the approaching separation.

"Do you see any prospect of returning for good?" asked the father a few evenings before the last, as they sat together, after supper,—the younger boys having retired to rest.

"Well, father," said William, "I should wish to do what I can for my brothers. Joe stands on his own feet now; as for Ted I think I may leave him to Joe, if you and mother consent to his going to sea; Joe is much more in the way than I am of hearing of an opening in that line. But then there's Samson, I don't know what you would wish about him? I am afraid he has not spirit enough for a farmer."

"No," said the father; "but I would sooner risk it, than have you stay away for him, till no one knows when!"

"Well, I need not do that, father; for if you thought he would do better in business, my uncle made me an offer before I came down, to take him on trial; and he might, I think, with his steady head, make a good man of business. If you liked him to come up to me this Christmas, I would see the boy fairly into his work, and then in another year I think I might hope to be a farmer again!"

It was agreed to give Samson leave to decide for himself the next day. William said he could never consent to bind down his brother to what he had felt so much, unless Samson was inclined for it himself; and Mrs. Smith said she should be satisfied if the boy made his own choice. So the next morning, after breakfast, the proposal was made to Samson. He waited a minute in grave consideration, then said with a deliberate tone—

"I should wish to come and see the place sometimes; but for the rest—I would as soon be up there as down here!"

Mrs. Smith looked out of the window, and tears started to her eyes.

"Never mind, mother," said William in a low voice, "there's many a heart wakes up from its home, that lay fast asleep in it!" But Mrs. Smith made no reply; she felt again the refluent wave of bitter memory, reminding her how little she had done to call forth and bind the hearts of her children to their home—their mother's dwelling-place! Yet William seemed as if he could love no other; but it might be only his father and the place he cared for! it was always for his father Joe talked of earning money! little Tim had seemed uneasy with her! and now Samson cared not whether he went or stayed! Oh, how bitterly around the heart flows sin's returning tide! But then back to the mother's memory came the first utterance of Rose on her return—the first words half smothered by her feeling, "Mother! oh, mother!" and looking round, as if to see whether the child who breathed them were still hers, she met the earnest eyes of Rose—bent in their full and tenderest expression upon her, as if only one thought were in her heart, and that one, how her mother would bear the decision for Samson to go! It was enough; the mother felt one child to be at least a gift from Heaven to her—a gift most undeserved; and her strengthened heart was ready to endure in patience and in hope; and to wait the influence of her now better feelings on all around. So it was decided for Samson to go.

Ted had stood by in breathless attention, while the fate of his brother was deciding; but the moment it was fixed for Samson to go, and farmer Smith had taken his hat and was gone out to his men, Ted exclaimed, "And what's going to be done with me? I mean to go to sea! Joe said he would find me a ship, and if he does not, I shall just run away and find one for myself!"

"Heyday!" answered William, "I shall look after Rover's old chain! How do you think you are to climb a mast?"

"I will just show you!" said Ted, springing into his tall brother's arms, then on his shoulder, his merry face looking down at his brother's as he asked, "Is not that something like it?"

"Well done!" answered William, "but there are no friendly arms on ship-board, I warn you!"

"Just you come off, then," said Ted, "and see me climb the barn-roof: I can do it all over! And if you and father don't find me a ship, I will find one for myself!"

"I tell you what, my little man," said William, stopping suddenly short, as Ted was leading him to the barn, "I shall not go a step farther, nor see you climb, till you have listened to me." So sitting down on a cart-shaft that rested on the ground, he made a prisoner of the impatient boy, and began his discourse.

"Now, Ted, I tell you what, if you talk so I shall expect to hear that you fall down from the barn-roof and kill yourself, before ever you see your ship!"

"Well, but I want to go to sea,—and father said I should,—and father never said Samson was to go to London,—yet he is to go, and I am not!"

"I would not have Samson in London if I could not trust him," replied William; "and if you were only a runaway—who would trust you? You must try to earn a ship, and then I have not the least doubt but we shall find you one, and then you will go on board to serve like a man, and not like a runaway slave!"

"But why may I not go now? I can never earn it, so it is not any use to try; and I can climb well enough, and that's all a sailor wants to know!"

"Yes, but you can earn it, and you will not be happy in it if you do not earn it!" said William.

"How can I earn it?"

"By trying to do your duty now—being a comfort while you are at home; and learning all you possibly can to make you worth taking on board ship."

"But I tell you I can climb—and that is all a sailor want's to know."

"If you think so, you are very much mistaken, and it is a very happy thing for you that the ship is not yet lying in the harbour waiting for you."

"Why, what do I want to know more than climbing?"

"What? why a sailor ought to know as many things as any one! The very first voyage you go you may be wrecked on some uninhabited island, and what use would you be then to yourself or to any one?—Nothing better than a poor helpless child! You must set to and learn the use of your hands for something more than climbing — a monkey can do that better than you already! but you hope to be a man, and I hope so too, and you must begin to act like one, and then I shall think we may look out for your ship."

"But, Will, what must I learn?"

"Why, go off to old Lewis, the basket-maker in the next village, and get him to teach you how to twist the willow withys, and don't you give over till you can make mother a basket strong enough to send her eggs to market in. And then go to old master Newson, and help him to make his wheels, and his barrows, and his carts. And then you must take to thatching, and learn how to bind a roof in dry—before you reckon yourself all ready for a life that may cast and leave you anywhere! And I advise you these next winter evenings, to get Rose to teach you how to work with a needle."

"So I will! and then, William, I can go to old Dawson, I know there's plenty of room for me at his stall, and I will be a cobbler, and mend and make shoes,—what fun! I will make haste and learn everything!"

"Yes, to be sure," replied William, "and then think of what use you might be! Why, you would be the last man on board ship to be parted with, if you could be of use for everything. And then, Ted, do you think I have told you all you would want to know?"

"I don't know," replied Ted, looking up, at William's earnest tone.

"What if there came a storm at sea, and the ship went down, and you went down to the bottom with it? do you think your spirit would rise, like a little diver, and know its way to the Holy Heaven—where Tim is gone to dwell?"

"Did Tim know the way?" asked Ted.

"Yes, don't you remember how he loved to pray, and to learn and repeat the texts and hymns Rose taught him, which tell of Jesus—Who is the way to Heaven?"

"Yes, I know that!" answered Ted.

"Then don't you think you will want to know

as much as little Tim knew, before you go on those great deep waters? And suppose you should find poor sailor boys, or men, who don't know the way to Heaven — you could teach them; and that knowledge would be the best of all, both for yourself and others.

"Yes, I dare say it might," replied Ted, "but I don't see that I can learn that."

"Not of yourself alone, but if you really try to learn, God will enable you both to know and to love it. Little Tim learned from Rose; would you like to go and see our Curate with me, and for me to ask him to take you into his class of boys, that you may learn that knowledge?"

"Yes, I should not mind that."

"Very well, then, we will go; and I think by the time we have found the ship, you will be ready for it, with knowledge to make you happy yourself, and a comfort and blessing, I trust, to others."

William returned with Joe to London, leaving Ted full of spirit for his trades; and received under the Curate's care, to learn that which hath the promise, not only of the life that now is, but of that which is to come. Ted inherited his mother's energy, and, being a general favourite, he found little difficulty in persuading the village trades-people to teach him something of their skill —some idea how their work was done, and their tools handled; besides—a refusal was not very easily given to one who had no idea of taking it. The Curate, in his walk through the village, would see his little scholar busy at the wheelwright's side; or look down upon his merry face in the cobbler's stall—intent with earnest gravity on mending some worn-out boot. Samson went to London at Christmas. And so passed away the village winter.

Old Willy's health had long been visibly declining; there were those who thought the old man would not see another spring, and not without reason—for in the frost of February he took to his bed, from which he never rose again. Widow Jones was nurse, Mercy his comfort, and Jem his earthly stay and dependence. Rose was often sent by her mother with something warm from the farm; and Mrs. Smith herself was not seldom seen making her way to the old man's cottage. Ted, to his own perfect satisfaction, had soled a pair of old Willy's boots, for which Dawson, the cobbler, said he should charge nothing, because the work was none of his! so Ted carried them home and set them down close by old Willy's bed—ready for him as soon as he might be able to get up; and from time to time the ministering boy looked in to see whether the old man had yet made trial of his new mended boots. But old Willy had trod the rough path of the world to its end; he had put off his shoes from his feet, and he needed to be shod no more, save with the preparation of the gospel of peace—which time and use, so far from impairing, can only serve to strengthen on the Heavenward pilgrim's feet.

At the approach of spring, notice arrived at the Hall, of the return of Mrs. Clifford and the young Squire, and immediate preparations were made. A request was sent that there should be no demonstration of joy on their return; it was to be as quiet and private as possible. The servants were to be arrayed in the garb of mourning; and every circumstance to mark the event, not as a family return, but as that of the widow and her fatherless son. The day was not made known, in order more effectually to prevent an assembling of the people. Jem now watched with anxious fear, lest the fast-waning life of old Willy should depart before his long-cherished wish had been granted—to see his young master again! Widow Jones and Mercy had for some time kept watch by day, and Jem slept in old Willy's room by night. And still the feeble lamp of life burned dimly on with that old man—as if no outward circumstance now affected its slow and gentle expiring. Widow Jones and Mercy were in the cottage, when at the sound of carriage-wheels Mercy ran to the door. It was a travelling carriage, and there could be little doubt that it was on its way to the Hall; but no one was visible within, no one looked out as it swiftly passed by old Willy's door. Could it be the young Squire, and the Lady of the Hall? Yes, Jem, when he came in the evening, brought word that it was said in the village they had arrived. Widow Jones had sat up through the previous night, and Jem was to keep watch through the first hours of this—till his mother, after necessary rest, should come and relieve him. The evening closed in, Jem drew the little window-curtain, lighted the candle, and opening the old man's Bible sat down to read. But he found it difficult to stay his thoughts on the sacred page, his mind was full of the young Squire's return—would he be altogether changed? Jem feared it must be likely he would—away so long, and in foreign parts, he could hardly return the same! Yet Jem believed the good were not given to change, he had heard his mother say so when he was a child; and surely the young Squire was good if any ever were! so it might be he would prove still the same. Then the question rose, would old Willy know him if he came to see him? Was there consciousness enough still left for the old man to know his hope fulfilled? and Jem looked round on old Willy in anxious inquiry. While his thoughts were thus busy, he heard a knock at the door; then a hand, to whom its latch seemed familiar, opened it; and a stranger gentleman looked in; Jem started up, but in a moment he knew the face, he knew the friendly smile, he knew the form, yes, he knew the very hand that was raised to silence his exclamation and then extended to him! Jem bowed his lowest bow, then took the offered hand, and grasped it in both of his, while such a light of sudden joy suffused his countenance that words were little needed. Laying his hat on the table, the young Squire turned to the bed where the old man lay with his eyes closed as if in slumber. He stood and looked on him in silence. Oh, then what a wave from memory's sea overflowed his heart!—the past, the long past became present again—he thought of his dream; and as vividly as then in his sleep did he now seem to see the bright angel who watched over the old man—the heir of glory. He thought of that time when his work of love had not even begun, he remembered how hard that work had seemed at first—then how pleasant; how the difficulty again grew worse than before—then brightened into joy. And with that remembrance came the thought of his father—how he had met him in his childhood's feelings, and made him possessor of the home where old Willy dwelt—the recollection of all passed before him, till he wiped away his starting tears, and turned round to Jem, saying softly, "He sleeps!"

"No, sir," Jem replied, "I doubt if he does! he lies now mostly in that quiet way—as if his doings with Earth were all over; and we don't disturb him, except for his food. But I will just speak to him, if you please, sir, for he has longed sore to see you, and maybe he will still have the knowledge to understand that!"

Jem went to the pillow, and stooping above it, said gently, "Daddy, look up! I say, daddy, look up and see who has come to you!"

The old man looked up, the voice had aroused him and called up his slumbering senses. Herbert knelt down by the bed; and the eye of the old man fell on him, and he gazed with that long earnest look that the departing spirit seems to cast back from a still lengthening distance—its last glance through the eyes that have been its earthly portals of vision. The old man gazed on Herbert, but did not speak. It might be he thought himself lost in some dream of a hope yet unfulfilled; however it might be, the old man gave no sign of recognition—save that fixed, earnest look on the face that now, after long years, was before him. Herbert in that sacred moment felt unwilling by the name so familiar to appeal to the old man—who seemed calmly departing; afraid to bring back before him the dim visions of Earth, when he was just landing in Heaven. So he thought of the words that old Willy most loved, and said in his clear softened tone, "Let not your heart be troubled; ye believe in God, believe also in me. In my Father's house are many mansions; if it were not so, I would have told you. I go to prepare a place for you. And if I go to prepare a place for you, I will come again and receive you unto myself; that where I am, there ye may be also." The old man's dying ear caught the joyful sound; he listened with clasped hands and eyes upraised, while Herbert thus performed for him the last sacred ministry his spirit needed on Earth. There was silence again, and the old man seemed to muse on the words he had heard. Then, as if waking afresh, he looked up to Jem, who stood still beside him, and called, in his feeble tone and words of endearment, "Jem, my poor boy!" Jem stooped to his pillow, and the old man said, "I have seen him! he is grown up a heavenly man! and he spoke those words from my Book that he had read me often and often before! I knew him, for the voice was his own!" Herbert still knelt, by the bed, but the old man ceased to discern him, his dim eyes now failed him. Then Herbert rose up, and taking his seat on the bed, he leaned over old Willy, and laid his hand gently on the old man's and said, "Willy, dear old Willy, your young master's here! I am he! don't you know me?"

Then the old man wept, and raising his hand, as had been his custom when feeling overpowered him, he said, "It is granted me then! my young master's come!" And looking through his tears to where Herbert sat before him, he said with calmer utterance, "I have waited for you! I knew you would come! and now I have seen you, I am ready to go! I heard those sweet words you spoke from my Book, and they have lifted me up to the mansions above—I am at the door, I shall soon be gone in, and you will come to me there! You sheltered me here, but the good Lord has sent for me home—His angels are come, but He let me stay till I had my last wish—to see you once more! Will you care for my Jem? and please let him have my Book to show him the Way; and the coat that you bought me—it will serve him many a year. And when I am gone, let them lay me to rest at the feet of my lady; I have stood at the foot of her tomb in winter and summer. I went there most days to look where she lay, and I would lie where I always have stood to keep watch over her; I know the angels keep sight of her grave, and they'll watch over me—whom she taught the way to Heaven where they dwell; she is sure to see me when they carry me in like the poor beggar she read to me of! She will know then how fast in my heart I have kept the name of my Saviour; long nights as I lay here, I say to myself, 'Jesus—my Saviour, Lord Jesus—my God!'—and it keeps me so close by the Heavenly gate that I have only been waiting for you! I leave you my blessing, dear young master, God grant you may know what the blessing of the poor man can be! 'tis the God above who makes the Poor's blessing rich, and with my dying breath I commend you to Him!"

Herbert had already bowed his head on the old man's hand, which his own hand still held; and at his parting blessing, the old man raised again his other hand in act of prayer, then, spent with the effort, it fell by his side, and he seemed to repose. Herbert at length rose, and spoke softly with Jem, and would have sent further assistants to watch through the night; but Jem said his mother had already had some hours of rest, and would be there by midnight, and he would rather be alone till then. So Herbert returned to the Hall: but a servant soon arrived at the cottage bringing warm cordials; Jem again roused the old man, to take some, and he well understood who had sent the warm cordial for him! then turning again to rest on his pillow, he slept; his breathing became stiller, till it ceased; and Jem, though watching beside him, knew not when he died.

Herbert called at the cottage the next day, and looked on the smile that lingered on the lips of the departed. Jem was away at the farm, but widow Jones and Mercy were there. Widow Jones took from a drawer a small bag of money, saying to Herbert, "I made my promise to the old man, sir, that I would give that for his burying; he said he considered it was right that he should make a provision for that."

"Keep it yourself," replid Herbert; "I shall lay him to his rest."

"Thank you, sir, I am sure," replied widow Jones, "but if you won't be offended, sir, I could not be satisfied to take it; because he had laid it all by, and I promised him to give it for that."

"Then let me have it," said Herbert, "and I will send it for Bibles to be given in heathen lands—that was what lay nearest his heart, and so in that way his own money shall embalm him!"

The winter's rain was over and gone, the flowers had appeared on the Earth, the time of the singing of birds was come, the voice of the turtle was heard in the land—then it was they laid the old man to his rest. Herbert walked on one side of the coffin, and Jem on the other, and the village mourners followed. They had dug the old man's grave, by the young Squire's direction, at the foot of the lady's tomb, and there, with the words of blessing and the tears of affection, they left him to his rest. Herbert lingered—Jem waiting near, at his desire; Herbert spoke not of the past, but it rose in fresh remembrance before him; till at last, turning slowly away from that hallowed spot, he descended the hill in heavenly converse with

Jem. The cottage was shut up, the young Squire kept the key, and the dwelling mourned for three months, in desolation, the life it had sheltered from birth, and now had lost from its shelter for ever.

X.

The Old Cobbler.

"Ready to give thanks and live,
On the least that Heaven may give."

"Godliness with contentment is great gain."—1 Tim. vi. 6.

We must return for our last visit to the town, and take a final leave of the childhood of little Jane. She had grown what her father called "a great girl:" she went daily, alone, to a good school in the town; and was often useful to her mother in the errands she could do for her. She still looked upon widow Jones and her granddaughter Mercy, the old people in the almshouse, and the lone old woman on the heath, as her particular friends; and now a whole family were to be added to the number. Jane heard of a poor old man in the town, a cobbler by trade, but scarcely able to earn food by his work. He had been a shepherd on the very heath where Jane's old woman lived; but he was obliged to give up keeping sheep, and now he earned his bread by mending shoes. Jane heard that he was as happy as he was poor: and she thought how delightful it would be to help him. So she told her mother all she had heard; and asked if she might not go herself, and take her own boots to be mended by him.

Mrs. Mansfield replied, "Yes, you may take them if you like: and tell the poor man to mend them up for giving away—he will be able to do them in a stronger way and for less money, or I should not think them worth doing at all. But are you sure you know exactly the place where he lives?"

"O yes, mamma, I know it exactly! I have been and looked down at it; only I would not go without your leave."

So Jane set forth with her boots in a little basket, and in her pocket a purse that had for some days held a piece of silver. Eager, rich, and happy, went the ministering child, gliding through the busy streets of the town! Her's was the joyous sense of power—how easily taught, how easily learned, and yet how often unthought of, unknown! She had love in her heart, work in her hand, and money in her purse—what could she not do! One thing was certain—she could help and comfort; and strong, and bright, and fearless in this undoubting faith she hastened on. She reached at last the narrow door at the top of the steep flight of steps that led to the little court where the cobbler dwelt. Jane stopped a moment, looked down into the strange place, then carefully descended the steep steps, made of red uneven bricks, and edged with rotting wood, till she arrived in safety at the bottom. The cobbler's dwelling was No. 2, and at the second cottage before her, Jane noticed the clean-washed bricks before the door: it looked like the entrance to a good man's dwelling. Jane gathered fresh pleasure at the sight, but now the shyness of a stranger came over her, and she knocked with some trembling at the door. A tall woman in a brown calico gown opened it, with a snow-white handkerchief under her dress, a cap of thick muslin as white, and her sick-looking face, almost as white also.

"Does Mr. May live here?" asked Jane.

"Yes, miss," said the woman with a curtsey, "will you please to walk in?" And Jane entered as neat a little dwelling as ever met a visitor's eye. A very small fire a few inches wide and deep, burned in the grate; over the fire was a high black mantel-piece; on one side the fire-place was a black closet door, and on the other another black door leading up-stairs; the walls were white-washed, and one little book-shelf suspended upon them, with a row of books in neatest order. There was a long hutch opposite the fire, and on it a store of large new-baked loaves; the floor was neatly sanded, and before the large lattice window stood the cobbler's low stall—not even a straggling leather or tool had escaped from it, to litter the brick floor; and before it sat the small old man, on a low round stool of homely manufacture, with his apron tied round him, busy at work. Two daughters rose up at Jane's entrance, and the old cobbler took his spectacles from his nose and looked round. Jane turned at once to him, and said, "I have brought a pair of boots, which mamma thought you might like to mend, and I was to tell you they are to be done for giving away."

"Thank you, miss, I am sure," said the cobbler; "it's well to know that, because you see then a patch outside, here and there, does not signify, and that's a deal less trouble to do, and lasts all the longer, because it dont wear out the old leather, like so many stitches as you must set into it for that fine particular mending that must be done for gentle folks." The old cobbler had risen up, and did not begin his response to the message till Jane was seated, so that Jane listened with a settled feeling to his long reply, which gave her complete satisfaction, as she had not quite liked to say they were to be mended for giving away! But she thought now how wise her mother was— who must have known all that, when she gave her the message! Though only a child had entered, the mother and daughters still stood, and Jane, uncomfortable at that, said, "I may stay a little while, if you are not busy, and can sit down?"

M. C.

The old cobbler fastened his spectacles on his nose, and was soon at his work again; but he seemed to feel that the responsibility of entertaining their guest rested with him, so he lost no time in going on to say, "It's a comfort, that many can little think, to see work come in at the door; for to sit here and earn the food one eats makes it seem to be doubly sweet; and I believe too that it does do you more good, for I believe that's the order God has written upon this world—that the bread of idleness shall do none the same good! And I am sure," said the cobbler, looking round, as he did for a moment at frequent intervals of his discourse, "I am sure, miss, we are thankful to you for the bringing it!"

"I liked to come," answered Jane, "I heard that your wife was ill."

"Well, miss," replied the cobbler, looking round kindly at his wife for for a moment, "she is never well. I do what I can, but one pair of hands can hardly keep four in food and clothing and house-rent, by shoe-mending! And she has been sickly now a long time. But, as I say, we do what we can, and there's the comfort of knowing that the trial is the will of the Lord. My poor girls there would be thankful to do what they could, but the Lord has not blessed them with the sense He has given to some: but still I say, if He is graciously pleased tc keep them from evil, and teach them the knowledge of Himself, why that's mercy enough to keep from fretting about the other. My poor boy is much the same, but he has got a place, and I hope he may keep it, for it brings in a little." Jane looked at the daughters, clean and neat as their mother, and almost as pale; they sat upright on chairs by the wall, and the unexpressive stare of their large round eyes gave evidence of some want of sense within. The father's face was very like his children's, except that in his eyes and on his lips was a smile as bright as a sunbeam; and the whole expression of his face when speaking was irradiated with Heavenly faith.

"Can your daughters do needlework?" asked Jane.

"Yes, miss, they can sew very neatly, when they can get it to do; and the eldest has been in a place, but she had not the strength to keep it. I hope, however, she may get the better of it again, and look for another situation before long, for it's trying to sit at home when there is not work or food; but, thank God, we have managed as yet, and we would do anything we could to keep the house and home together."

"You have bread now!" said Jane, in a tone expressive of her pleasure at the sight of the large loaves on the hutch.

"O yes, miss, and I don't know that we have ever been a day altogether without! The bread that you see will all wait for a fortnight. We always bake one fortnight under another; that's a rule we never break when we can possibly buy the flour, for no one would believe the difference it makes—how far a little bread will go to satisfy your hunger, when once it begins to turn mouldy! My wife can shew you, we are now beginning the last fortnight's bread, and that must hold out, or we should never be able to manage at all!" This was said in the earnest, cheerful tone of one who had discovered a fortunate secret of sufficiency; the wife and daughter removed the hot loaves, opened the hutch, and shewed the hard-looking bread now coming into use. Jane was distressed; it was a study in poverty new to her, and the thought of this constant denial of pleasant food fell more heavily on her heart than would the knowledge of the occasional want of bread—a want, the experience of which she never knew, and therefore the suffering of which she would not fully have realized. The cobbler through his spectacles read the look of distress on the face of Jane, and in a moment turning his quick bright glance from his low stool again upon her, he said, in a tone of cheerful comfort, "There's no riches promised us here, if we be the Lord's; only the riches of faith and the riches of His blessing—and thanks be to Him, we have them; so we can say, He is faithful that promised! And 'tis my belief there's nothing makes the true riches increase so fast as trial does; so we must beware how we fret at it, lest we lose our best gain along with it!" Jane looked at the beaming face of the cobbler, with its kind and lingering expression of inquiry on her—as if to see whether he had removed the cloud he had cast over her, and she thought she had never seen any one look so happy as that poor man; and her heart grew warm again in the sunshine of his faith—for the sudden shock of what she heard about the bread had chilled her with distress.

"Are you never unhappy because you have not better food?" asked Jane.

"Well, miss, trouble is always ready enough to spring up; it's got its root in my heart, and so it will have as long as there's any sin there for it to grow in; but blessed be God, I know what to do with it; I never let it hold up its head long; I take it right away to our Saviour in prayer, and I leave it with Him, for I believe he knows better than I do how to manage with it; and so sure as I persevere in doing that, it comes right in the end, or I come right out of it."

Jane listened, and she loved to listen; for that old man's faith was truly making sunshine in the shade of his deep poverty. But now she began to think that perhaps she ought not to stay any longer; so, rising up to go, she slipped her piece of silver, which she had managed to get unseen from her purse, into the cobbler's hand, saying softly, "Will you take that little present from me?" and then, in a minute more, she was climbing the steep steps that led out of the court.

Jane waited in hope of some more shoes needing repair, and it was not long before her mother—who never forgot a case of want when once made acquainted with it, called her, and packed into a basket some of the children's shoes, which she told Jane she might take to her cobbler. So Jane set out on the pleasant errand. As she descended the high steps she heard some one singing; it was a bright spring day, and the cobbler's lattice window was open; Jane felt sure the voice came from there; as she passed the window, it stopped. Jane delivered the work she had brought into the hands of the cobbler, and then sat down on the chair he had set for her near his stall, quite disposed to linger in the tempting-looking cottage, now lighted up by the spring's sweet sunshine.

"Do you sing at your work?" asked Jane.

"Well, miss, I do amuse myself a little that way sometimes," said the old man, going on as fast as possible with his mending, "I find it keeps troublesome thoughts out, and cheers my spirits up. I was singing a verse as you came, that's seldom long from my thoughts," and the cobbler took off his spectacles, and looked up with his face of unchanging sunshine and said,—

"Though vilely clad, and meanly fed,
And, like my Saviour, poor,
I would not change my Gospel bread,
For all the worldling's store!"

Now Jane was surprised at the cobbler's happiness, and could not quite understand why he should seem to be the happiest of all the good people she knew; so she said, "Every one who loves God is not so happy as you are?"

"Well, miss," replied the cobbler, "perhaps it is not given to all alike,—we see a deal of those differences in the Bible. It pleases God, I believe, to try His people some one way, and some another. I am very poor, but maybe there's another who is not—then he must have his trial some other way; let it be as it will, each must have a trial!" said the cobbler looking up over the top of his spectacles earnestly at Jane, as if anxious to impress that truth on her mind, "All must have a trial some way—because it is written, 'Ye must through much tribulation enter the kingdom of Heaven!'"

"But," asked Jane, "is it not very difficult to be always happy?"

"Well, miss," answered the cobbler, without pausing in his busy labour, "I should soon be dull enough if I were left to myself; but I will tell you what I find the best help, I always try to keep a flame of praise lit up in my heart, and that burns up the dross of unbelief and discontent in a won derful way! That's one reason why I so often take to singing a hymn—when I find that flame of praise is getting low, and I can only work on, and so little coming in often for my work when it is done, then I get singing some hymn of praise to that Saviour who worked out my salvation at at such a cost as His own blessed life, and gives it to me without money and without price; and then when praise to Him kindles up in my heart, it burns up the discontent in no time. And then, dear me, what mercies come in! It was only last night I lay awake thinking entirely of our Mary; you see, miss, she is the youngest, and I have had many an anxiety about her, not but what she is a good girl to us, but she is very silent, and I was afraid whether the love of her Saviour was in her heart. Well, as I lay awake last night, I kept praying that the Lord would give her grace to choose the better part, like Mary we read of in the Scriptures, but I did not say anything to her; well, this morning she said to me, 'Father, there was a text in my mind last night that I could not seem to forget, "Mary hath chosen the better part, that shall never be taken from her,"—I hope I shall do that! father.' Now what a mercy that was; who could but know that must be the Lord's doing!"

It was no wonder that Jane loved to visit the cobbler's bright cottage. There she saw faith, not so much contending with difficulties as triumphing over them, and its victory could not but appear beautiful, even to the eyes of a child. One day, as Jane was looking at a hymn-book, she suddenly caught sight of the very same verse that the old cobbler had repeated to her as the one he had been singing. Jane showed it to her mother with the greatest interest; and her mother always quick to meet and strengthen every pure and hallowed feeling, found an embossed card she had somewhere laid by, and in her plainest writing copied the favourite verse, in the centre of the card; then finding four little brass nails, and showing Jane how to cut up a piece of scarlet cloth in small rounds to fix the nails into, she gave it into Jane's possession, who went the next day, after her morning school, by her mother's leave, to carry the treasure. She stood up in a chair, and nailed it herself with the cobbler's little hammer over the mantel-piece, while all the family stood admiring; and there the cobbler, whenever he looked up, was reminded of his hymn of praise. Jane gave so warm an account of the feeling called forth by the card upon the walls, that her mother said, "If you save up your pence for a month, I will show you what more you can do to adorn the cottage." Jane could not imagine what fourpence could do to adorn her old cobbler's walls; she tried to find out, but she could not guess, and her mother still kept back the secret. At last the fourth Saturday came, and Jane was possessor of fourpence. "Now, mamma, what can it be? do tell me!" "You shall go out with me, and then you will see!" said her mother. So Jane went out with her mother, and when Mrs. Mansfield had accomplished her business, she took Jane to a stationer's shop, and asked for some pasteboard; she chose three penny sheets, dark purple on the wrong side, and white on the right; then Mrs. Mansfield asked for some tissue paper, and chose a penny sheet of lilac colour. "Now, Jane," said Mrs. Mansfield, "you have spent your fourpence, and this afternoon you shall see what you can do!" On their return, Mrs. Mansfield looked out with Jane some of the most interesting pictures on the Church Missionary papers; then making some paste, she bade Jane put on her pinafore, and laying the nursery ironing-board on the nursery table, Mrs. Mansfieled showed Jane how to divide the large sheets of pasteboard in half, then to cut the tissue paper in broad strips, and paste it round the margin of the pasteboard, laying the Missionary picture in the middle; then pressing them under something heavy, and large enough to cover them, they looked, when dry, like pictures mounted on coloured cardboard, and the broad lilac margin made the effect very pretty. Jane was delighted with her work, and the next week, when the pictures were quite dry, her mother provided the scarlet cloth to be cut into very small rounds for each nail, and four nails for each picture, there being six pictures, and Jane carried a hammer at the bottom of her little basket, for fear the old cobbler's small wooden hammer should not prove sufficient; and attended by the cobbler's wife and daughters, while the old cobbler looked up from his work continually, Jane put up the pictures to the pleasure and admiration of all. Then the old cobbler stood up and looked round with delight—on scenes that told of the triumphs of his own pure and Heavenly faith over the dark and cruel superstitions of idolatry. From that time it was a favourite amusement with Jane, to save up her weekly pence and make pictures to adorn the walls of all her poor friends.

And now we must say farewell to Jane in her childhood. We leave her gathering around her the hearts of the poor. And He who guides the sparrow's fall, guided her steps, so that never breath of evil, or sight of sin, fell on her childhood's ear or eye, among the Poor.

XI.

Black Beauty.

"It grew up together with him, and with his children; and was unto him as a daughter."—2 Sam. xii. 3.

When three months had passed away, the young Squire went alone to old Willy's cottage; he stayed some time in the house, then walked in the garden, and seemed engaged in a general consideration of the place. The next day workmen arrived, and the young Squire went to meet them. Then began pulling down and building up; the front of the cottage remained as it was, the room in which old Willy sat by day and slept by night was untouched, but other rooms were added behind, till the dwelling rose with its three chambers above, its back-kitchen and little dairy, and outhouses, complete. Some said it was going to be turned into a farm; but no, it was a simple cottage still, too large for one person, but with every comfort for a family. The young Squire often walked down to the spot, looking with interest on all, and giving his directions to the workmen.

Meantime the summer months were gliding by Snowflake and Jet again drew the pony-carriage, and Herbert again drove his mother out; and still sometimes Mrs. Clifford would call at a cottage, but more generally she only stopped in passing, to make kind inquiry! it was evident that general intercourse with others was, as yet, an effort to her. But one day she stopped at widow Jones' door, and went in. Mrs. Clifford had never forgotten Mercy—the child in whom Miss Clifford had always taken more interest than in any other; and Mrs. Clifford, knowing her to be of an age for service, and remembering her delicate look, was afraid lest any place of common work should prove beyond her strength, so she called on widow Jones to ask whether she had any wish about her grand-daughter that she could be aided in. Widow Jones replied that she had long been on the lookout for a situation for Mercy; the field-work was too much for her, she had not the strength for it —and that was her fear about service, but she believed she must make inquiry for a place in the town before another winter came on. Hearing this, Mrs. Clifford offered to take Mercy, and have her trained under her own maid, adding, "I should have her a good deal with me, she would have to read to me, and to carry out many little plans I may not feel able to undertake myself, in the village. I believe her to be capable of this, and if it meets your wish, I shall be quite willing to try her." This proposal was received with overflowing gratitude by widow Jones; and when Mercy heard of it, with delight by her. To live still in her own village, near her grandmother, and to wait on Madam—all this was more than hope could have believed, or imagination pictured! So Mercy went to service at the Hall, to wait on Mrs. Clifford, and be trained under her maid.

When September hung its ripe fruit upon the trees in old Willy's garden, the cottage stood complete; the bricklayers, and carpenters, and thatchers, and glaziers, and painters were gone; the door was again locked, and the place stood silent and peaceful. Then early one summer evening, just as Jem returned home from his work at the farm, the young Squire called at his cottage, saying, "I came to ask you and your mother to come and see the dear old man's dwelling. I have had it enlarged; and you always took so much interest in it, that I wish to shew it to you myself."

Widow Jones put on her bonnet, and walked up the lane with her son Jem and the young Squire. The sun was setting, and his parting beams fell upon the cottage-roof, and gilded the garden trees. The young Squire crossed the garden-stile—the very same that used to be—then turning round, he said with a grave smile to Jem, "Do you remember the dark morning when you and I first crossed that stile together?" "It was a good morning, sir, for him that dwelt within!" said Jem; and on they passed.

The young Squire unlocked the door, and they went in. There was the same look about the open fire-place; the very chair old Willy always sat in —with its crimson cushion—was there; there stood the little table, and the very stool on which the young Squire used to sit. The bed was gone, and in its place stood a bureau, and a larger table, and chairs round the room—while flowers in pots bloomed in the window. "What do you think of it?" asked the young Squire, as Jem and his mother looked round with wondering eyes. "'Tis made wholly beautiful, I am sure!" said Jem. "There is not the cottage like to it in the place!" said widow Jones.

"Then, Jem, what do you say to being my tenant, and bringing your old mother to live here in comfort?"

"Well, sir, I am afraid I should fail more in the doing than the saying, so far as that is concerned; my best wages could never clear the rent of such a place as this!"

"And I suppose," said the young Squire, "you would be as hard as my dear old Willy himself, to be persuaded that a house could be honestly tenanted without the payment of money! But you need not fear robbing me when I say you shall pay me no rent, for I hold this dwelling a sacred place, for many reasons, and so long as I can find a faithful heart to inhabit it, I never mean to let it for money! I make it your home now, and your mother's till such time as you may receive notice to quit it—which will not be with my desire, so long as life is granted you, if you are enabled to maintain the same character as that which wins my regard for you now. You will find the upper rooms furnished as well as this. The furniture is all your own, I purchased it for you: the house and land you hold as my tenant—in proof of which you may always send up to the Hall the first dish of rosy apples you gather from the trees I planted! There is a small field, that was part of the little place when bought; I let it to the farmer who had hired it before, old Willy having no use for it; but I have now attached it to the cottage, and had a gate made into it from the garden: you can let it or use it, as you like, only seeing that it is kept in grass, and not dug up without my consent. And may old Willy's God grant you to live to as blessed and peaceful an old age as he enjoyed beneath this roof!" Widow Jones and her son were filled with surprise and gratitude. The Squire let them speak their own broken words of thankfulness, that they might not afterwards feel distressed at having said nothing. And then talking a few minutes more with them, and telling widow Jones that he should request his mother to let her grand-daughter be sent to them the next day to help them move in, he left them with the key in their possession.

The move was soon effected—where everything was prepared beforehand for use and comfort. Widow Jones sold off most of her old furniture, saying there was scarce a piece of it that was fit so much as to see inside of such a place as the Squire had prepared for her Jem! and there, with Mercy's help, they slept in peace the following night: widow Jones only expressing her fear, as to how she could ever bring her mind to the care of such things as stood on every side there—look which way you would! When the young Squire went to college in October, he left Jem quietly settled in his new abode. The village rejoiced in the good fortune of honest Jem; for Jem was, as may be supposed, a general favourite. Was he not always ready to lend a helping hand, to tender some kindly office in sickness or trouble, and at all times to speak a pleasant word? None but the bad could have failed to look kindly on Jem! But among the general pleasure, none was more warmly expressed than Mrs. Smith's; her regard for both mother and son seemed to make her pleasure in the event double: and never could honest labourer, and faithful servant, and dutiful son, have entered a new abode with more pleasant feeling to himself and others—than honest Jem, when he called the home of old Willy his own!

At the farm, William's return had been anxiously looked for, this year: but when the time drew near he wrote word to his father, that though very sorry to be absent longer, he did feel a wish to wait one year more. His uncle, he said, would be glad to detain him, and offered to raise his salary again—but he did not feel bound on that account; still there were reasons that would make him glad of another year, and though he felt the disappointed hope more, he was sure, than any one else could, yet, if his father were willing, he certainly should wish to stay till the following July, when he hoped to be down in time to put the first sickle to the corn! Samson was getting on well in his uncle's business and favour; Joe was as happy as possible, and plainly giving satisfaction in the merchant's office—and by next year Joe expected to find a ship for Ted. So the hope of the parents was still deferred; and a short visit from their three sons, was all they could that year enjoy. William said nothing as to his reason for wishing to remain longer in London; but everything seemed going on well for the three brothers; and it was not difficult for farmer Smith to believe that to have William to watch over the other two was a great security for them.

In the following winter the old Clergyman died.

Much anxiety was felt in the village as to whether the Curate would remain; the anxiety of Mrs. Smith equalled that felt by farmer Smith and Rose, and great was the universal joy when it was known that Mrs. Clifford had presented the living to the Curate, and that now the villagers might hope he would live and die among them. The late Clergyman's widow remained some months in the rectory, and everything went on as before; till one day farmer Smith returned from market with an unusually clouded brow.

"I never saw you look more like bad news!" said Mrs. Smith, "what has happened?"

Farmer Smith was silent.

"Come now," said Mrs. Smith, "bad will be none the better for waiting! I may as well know to-day as to-morrow."

"It's only the horse!" said farmer Smith. "I saw a paper in the town, and there's to be a sale at the rectory, and Black Beauty is in the list."

"Well," replied Mrs. Smith, "he is none of your's now! and you can't take up with vexing over the sale of other people's creatures. Not but what I am sorry enough myself, but I have seen the good of his going since, and you must think of that. If Will laid the first stone of Joe's good fortune, it was the horse helped you to set him on it, you could not have done it without him. I am sure I made sin enough of it before, so I have reason to bear with it now. I am only thankful *the child* does not know of his going—he used to count so of seeing the creature pass by! but he is better off; and we, why we must take the rough with the smooth as it comes, and be thankful there's One who can make them both 'work together for good,' as the Minister tells us."

Farmer Smith felt relieved, for he had dreaded the telling his wife, or her knowing that the favourite horse was to be put up to the highest bidder. The young Squire was absent at college; and many a time farmer Smith thought, had he but been at the Hall there was little doubt that he would have bought the favourite, and then the creature would but have exchanged one good stable for another, still in sight of its first possessors. But the young Squire was away, so there was no prospect but that of soon looking his last on Black Beauty.

No further mention was made of the subject, till a day or two after, Ted rushed in exclaiming, "Mother, where's father? there's to be a sale at the rectory, and Black Beauty's down in the list! the bill is up on the blacksmith's shop—I saw it myself!"

"Well, child, the rector's lady has as much right to sell the horse as your father had—it was his then, and it's her's now."

"What, don't you mind about it then, mother?"

"Mind! child, what's the use of minding? I have vexed too much already for the poor beast! Don't you say a word to your father about it; I shall mind that if you do; let him forget it if he can."

"But, mother, father can't forget it! How can he forget, when he must hear and know all about it?"

"Well, don't you say a word to make him think the more; you try and make the best of it, not the worst—that's what you have to do."

"I know what I shall do," replied Ted, "I shall just write off and tell William!"

"No, that I do forbid," said Mrs. Smith; "for why in the world should you want to worry him with it? do you think he has not felt enough about it already?"

"Yes, mother, but then I know William has some money; I am quite sure of that, and a great deal too, for when I asked him if he had not last time he was down, he said, 'What you would call a great deal perhaps!' so I know he has, and then he could just send and buy Black Beauty away from them all!"

"That does not signify," replied Mrs. Smith. "If William has money, he has earned it hardly enough, and I would not for the world have it taken from him to buy back a horse."

"Well mother, William does not care for money,

I am sure, for he said when I asked him if he had not got a great deal, that he would have given all up over and over again to be only yard-boy on father's farm—if there had been none but himself he had to think of! so I am sure he can't care for money! and everybody knows how he cared for that horse!"

"Never mind, child, it's plain enough he did not wish to be after buying him back, or he could have said as easy as not, 'If there's a sale, you might let me know!' but he never said a word about it in any letter, and if we write to him about it, why it will put him up to do it just to please us, and I would not have that on any account. I will not have a word written to any one of them till the sale is over; you remember I have said it!"

"Well, mother, if I must not speak to father, nor William, I declare I will go off to the sale and see after the horse myself! and I will speak a word to whoever buys him—let it be who it will, if it's no more than to tell them what our Minister told us in our class—it may stick by them, and fright them a little, if they don't use him as they should! I would not have him bought and led off, and no one to speak a word for him for anything!"

"Very well," replied Mrs. Smith, "so long as you keep to what our Minister says, you are safe enough!" And Ted satisfied at having at last fixed upon something he might do, grew more composed on the subject, and when alone with his father, he said, "Never you mind, father, about Black Beauty's being sold off again, I have just got a word to say to whoever buys him that may be of good use to the horse; I mean to be up at the sale, and see all about it, and then I can tell you, father!" And the thought of this seasonable address that was to be made to the buyer of Black Beauty, with the care necessary in composing and recomposing it to make it as brief and forcible as possible, changed the prospect of the approaching sale into an event of effort and interest, rather than of distress to Ted.

The morning of the sale arrived. "Mother," said Ted, "I must be off now, and I want my best jacket, no one will care for me if I don't look something respectable." So Mrs. Smith brought Ted his best jacket, which was of dark blue, having been his particular request as most suitable for one who was soon to be a sailor; arrayed in this, with his round straw hat on the side of his head, and his little cane in his hand, he set off to the sale. "Never you mind, father!" said Ted, as he stopped to speak to his parent on the green slope from the house, "I am off to the sale, just to do what can be done, and then I will come home and tell you. And there's sure to be good come of it, father, though we may never know it, for the Minister says, when the right thing is done, if people don't think of it at first, they will sooner or later; and I know just what he said about those who have to do with dumb creatures; so never you mind, father, I am now off for the sale! Tell mother not to think about dinner for me, there's no saying when I shall be back." "Take care what you are after!" said the father. But off ran the ministering boy to watch over Black Beauty, and speak the word of warning he had heard from the Minister's lips, to whoever might purchase the horse.

It was a heavy day to farmer Smith—this second sale of the favourite horse, close by his own door, and he not able to purchase it back, nor now to have any control over the hands into which it passed! The creature had been born and reared on his farm, had played with his children, fed from their hands, he had himself broken it in for use, and it would leave its food or its pasture at any time at the first sound of his voice—the after-tie may be strong between master and steed, but it is on the farm where the creature is born, and reared, and trained, that the feeling becomes all but a family bond!

Mrs. Smith took the event more quietly, her heart had been broken up by the bitter anguish of remorse—remorse for years of pride and self-will;

and though the balm of Heavenly love may bind up such broken hearts, yet must the surface-changes of life have but comparatively little power to distress—where sorrow so far deeper still lies within. Yet Mrs. Smith did feel it; and the point in which it touched her most, was her sense of what the sorrow of little Tim would have been—to have had his favourite sold away a second time, where he could never see him pass. But Mrs. Smith spoke not of this! she had learned to endure in silence, conscious of the past—when her personal annoyances were always made a subject of distress for others; so she now made an effort to hide her own feeling and comfort those around her. Rose saw her father's grave expression of face, and stepping out beside him after dinner, said, "Never mind, father, I think it's better the horse should be taken quite away before Will comes home, or he would always be seeing him, and then you know, father, perhaps he could not help wishing for him, and that would be wrong now he is sold away; and it would be vexing to William, and to Joe—if he knew that William could not help wishing him back; so I think it's best, father!"

"So it is, Rose, I dare say, if I could but be sure of his being well off!"

"But, father, God made the creatures; and when we can't take care of them any longer we must leave them to Him! I am sure, father, you did the best you could, and then if we don't feel satisfied, that looks as if we could not trust God Almighty; and you know it says in the Bible, the sparrow does not fall to the ground without our Heavenly Father!"

"So it does, Rose; I will think of that. Oh, if my mother could but hear how you comfort me! But I have a hope now, that I shall show you to her some day in Heaven, and tell her how her prayers were all answered, though she never knew it." So farmer Smith passed on with livelier step to his men, and Rose went back to iron at her mother's side.

Ted had not returned to dinner; and now his mother, each time she paused in her work and set the iron down upon the stand, gave a glance from the window.

"I can't think what the child is stopping after, all this time!" at length said Mrs. Smith.

"I daresay Black Beauty came near the end of the sale," replied Rose, "and he said he should not stir from the place till he saw what became of him."

Mrs. Smith said no more; only looking from time to time along the distant road. Four o'clock —five o'clock passed, and Rose prepared the tea the ironing was finished and all cleared away, the table was set, the toast made, farmer Smith came in, but no Ted appeared.

"I cannot think what the boy is after!" said Mrs. Smith. "I wish you would just step and see; and tell him he must come home. I would not have him stay after dark among a set of horse-dealers for anything!"

Farmer Smith took his hat and went; and Mrs. Smith watched at the window—watched till she saw him returning alone. "Where's the child?" asked Mrs. Smith, "I wish enough you had brought him!"

"I don't think he will take any harm," replied farmer Smith. "I saw Beetlebright, the horse-dealer, there, and I asked him to have an eye on the boy, who was in the very thick of it, amongst them all, looking on as earnest as possible: I could not catch a sight from his eye; and Beetlebright told me the horse was coming on directly, so I came off, for I could not stand to see him led up! But I was not sorry I went, for I heard some good news!"

"Did you?" asked Mrs. Smith; and her tone betrayed how far she was from indifference on the subject.

"Yes, Beetlebright told me he knew who had given orders to have the horse purchased, and I might be sure he would have a good master, if ever he had!"

"Well, that's a comfort," said Mrs. Smith, "I am sure I am thankful enough! Did he say who?"

"No, he turned off at that; and I thought no doubt he would not be free of speaking beforehand, and I heard them call for the horse, so I came off."

Upon this, Mrs. Smith, and Rose and her father sat down to tea, but with more feeling than appetite.

"Just look here, Miss Rose!" said Patience, stepping quickly up to the door of the family kitchen, which always stood open.

All ran to the window, being ready for any alarm. There came the boy, in blue jacket and straw hat, mounted on Black Beauty, as large as life, and as steady as Time, stepping down the old familiar hill, the home-road to the farm, which he had never trod since the day that Joe led him away. All hurried out from the door: Rose flew down the sloping green to the valley at the foot of the hill, where Black Beauty, at meeting her, stopped of his own accord, and arched his neck, and put his nose into her hand.

"Now, Rose, that will do; don't you see I want to be off to father!" said Ted. And Black Beauty started on the accustomed canter along the path up the greensward that led to the wicket gate of the garden.

"Do go and see," said Mrs. Smith "what the boy is after!"

But farmer Smith stood still with Mrs. Smith

beside the garden-gate, at which, in a minute more, Black Beauty made a stand.

"What in the world have you been after, boy? What are you doing with the horse?" asked Mrs. Smith; while Rose came breathless from her run, and stood beside. But now Black Beauty's turn was come to give expression to his feeling,—he stood again upon home-ground, close to his master, who had never spoken to him since the parting day; he rested his head upon his master's shoulder, stepped from side to side, and courted the caress first of one and then the other—while all seemed to fail in its power to express the noble creature's joy. The labourers were returning home from the farm, laden with their implements and baskets, and they gathered wondering around. Jem and the yard-boy, and Patience too, were there—all looking intent on the mystery; while Mrs. Smith hastily repeated her inquiry,—

"What in the world are you after, boy! Make haste, I say, and speak it out!"

"Now, mother," said Ted, seated like a chieftain on his charger, "don't look as if you thought it must be wrong because I have done it!"

"Done what?" said Mrs. Smith, "what have you done?"

"Why, brought the horse home, mother!"

"But how came you by him? that's what I want to know!"

THE RETURN OF BLACK BEAUTY.

Ministering children Vol. II, p. 216.

"Well, mother, I did not steal him—though you look as if you were afraid I had; nor beg him, nor borrow him; he was given me right away for father as I stood there!"

"Who by?" asked farmer Smith, anxiously and earnestly.

"Why, I don't know, father, only it was the man who bought him, so I suppose he had a right to give him if he liked!"

"I am afraid there's some mistake in it!" said farmer Smith, seriously,—looking along the road to see if explanation, clearer than his boy's, might be coming there,—but no one was in sight.

"Well—now, father, you listen, and I will just tell you," said Ted, still seated on the creature—yet restless with its joy. "As soon as ever they led up the horse there was a man came and stood near where I was; he seemed, I thought to be thinking of buying, and I wished he might; for I liked the look of him. Well, they kept bidding, and I got in such a way, for the man seemed ever so many times as if he would let him go, and he kept so quietly at it, that at last I did not know who had the horse; but I found he was gone down to some one, so I kept asking, 'Who has him? who has him?' and they pointed to this man. So I watched my opportunity when he was pretty well alone, and then I went up and just said what I had to say to him, as to his care of the horse! Well, he listened, and when I had done, he said, 'You come along with me, and see what you think of my usage!' so I went with him, and he never said a word more, but unpacked this saddle and bridle—only you see, father, what a saddle it is!" said Ted, tumbling himself off and lifting up the lappets, more thoroughly to display the saddle's excellence.

"Well, child, what then?" asked his mother.

"Why, when he had done putting them on, and seeing they were all right, he said, "Now, little master, have you a mind to ride?" and before I knew what to say, he had lifted me up. O how the good creature did paw the ground when I was once upon him! he knew me as well as anything! and thought he was coming off here, I know he did!"

"Well, child, but go on!" said Mrs. Smith.

"Dear me, mother, I don't know any more! only when the man had lifted me on, he said, 'You go and preach your sermon to your father, for he is the owner of this horse now; and you tell him that if he does not know how to take care of him he has a son that can teach him! And I will be down after you presently, when I have settled some other business.'"

"Was it Beetlebright, the horse-dealer?" asked farmer Smith.

"I don't know, father, but I think I have seen him before in town."

"But did he not say a word of who sent him?"

"Why he sent him, father! he bought him and sent him!"

"Nonesense, child; a horse-dealer would never make me such a present!"

"Here's some one now coming down the road, sir," said one of the men. They all watched; and farmer Smith soon descried the substantial figure of Beetlebright the horse-dealer, who made his way to the assembled group.

"I am afraid," said farmer Smith, stepping forward, "we are under some little mistake in stopping the horse at our gate!"

"Not a bit of it," replied the horse-dealer, "if you can trust that hand-writing, and I think it's as good and honest a hand as I have seen for many a day!" So saying, the horse-dealer gave a sealed letter to farmer Smith, who opened it and read:

"Dear Father,

"It was my sorrow to cost you your favourite horse; you did not spare him, neither did William, and now it is my joy to have earned him back again. I have been so afraid I should not get money enough before—for some reason or other—he might be sold off! I have never spent so much as a sixpence, no, nor a penny, I think, that I could do without; and now I have twenty pounds in hand over and above what you had for him, so I am sure of it now. I hope I am thankful, I am sure I think I am. Don't let a word be said to William, but when he comes home let the horse be taken to meet him.—Be sure you don't let him know till then! My love to mother, and Rose, and Ted.

"Your affectionate and dutiful son,

"JOSEPH SMITH."

Farmer Smith put the letter into his wife's hand, and turned to the horse to hide his feeling.

"Well, I suppose it's all right?" said the horse-dealer. "Here's my commission too, with the order for the new saddle and bridle;" and he put an open letter into farmer Smith's hand. "As to what your son says upon paying my charge on the commission, that's all paid already in the pleasure of the job—I can say I never had a pleasanter; and if such a lad does not turn out well, I don't know who will!"

"Who's done it, father?" asked Rose.

"Why Joe himself!" said her father; "he says he has never spent a sixpence he could help, for fear he might not have the money ready when an opportunity of buying the creature might come!"

"Well done, Joe!" said Ted. "I'll be up to you, when I'm a sailor though!"

"It's master Joe! it's master Joe has done it himself!" was repeated among the men; and cast ing a pleased expressive look at the father of such a son, they began to disperse to their homes, to tell there how master Joe had never rested till he bought back the black horse to his father's stable! Mrs. Smith gave back the letter to her husband, and turned within doors, glad at that moment to escape observation.

"Well, you will be thinking, I suppose, of leading him off to his stable?" said the horse-dealer. "I wish you joy of him, and twenty times more of such a son! And then I will just step in with you, for I am altogether done up with my day's work." Ted led the horse, and farmer Smith followed, and Jem to unsaddle him, and Rose followed also. Ted made all haste to give the horse a feed, but the creature, when he stooped to receive it, looked round, as if something were missing. "Come, Black Beauty, eat!" said Ted, impatient to give the first food; but the horse, while he stooped his head in obedience, still lifted his large eye, and looked to the door.

"Look, father, what's the matter?" said Ted. "Black Beauty won't eat!"

"Never mind," said Rose, "don't say a word, he is watching for little Tim! Here put his food in the manger, he will eat when we are gone; and come in to tea, do, Ted; you have had nothing since breakfast!"

So Ted spread out the food in the manger, and

followed his father and the horse-dealer, with Rose in to tea.

"What's the matter, mother?" asked Ted, as his mother stooped to tuck him up in his little bed that night.

"Nothing, dear," answered his mother, "only I was thinking how good Joe had been!"

"Well, mother, I would wait till Joe was bad, before I cried about him!" said Ted.

"Ah, Ted," replied his mother, "perhaps you may know some day what it is to shed a tear for goodness you don't deserve; for the Lord's goodness, if not for man's!"

"Was that all you were thinking of, mother?" asked Ted, concerned at the sight of his mother's tears.

"Well, I was thinking of little Tim, and how delighted he would have been to see the horse come back!"

"Well, mother, you need not cry about him; we read in our class to the Minister, how they ride on white horses in Heaven! and he is better off there, mother."

"So he is, dear!" replied Mrs. Smith; and kissing her boy, she left him to sleep on his pillow, and turned away to think of her children on Earth, and her youngest in glory in Heaven.

At last came the bright harvest month, July; and before the sickle was put to the corn, William was to return. And Joe got leave of a few days' absence also, having obtained a berth for Ted on board a merchant-ship. The two brothers travelled outside the coach. O what a day was that for William—all his best hopes fulfilled, and he returning, after so many years of absence, to live at home again and farm his father's land! Chesnut was put in the gig, and Ted was to ride Black Beauty, for William, with the new saddle and bridle. All day the farm had been in commotion; Patience scrubbing and cleaning the always clean house; Mrs. Smith baking her largest variety of best approved viands; Rose hanging the new little curtains she had made at the window of what was now to be William's room; men and boys getting all things in their best order—in preparation for Master William's return; while Ted devoted himself exclusively and entirely to the grooming of Black Beauty. Then came the starting-time, when farmer Smith drove off in the gig, and Ted--in blue jacket and straw hat—on Black Beauty, who ambled and capered along as if he knew it to be a festive occasion.

"Ah! you good old fellow," said Ted, "you little think who you will have to bring home again with you!"

Mrs. Smith watched from the door till the gig and the horse were out of sight, then turned within to hasten preparations with Rose. The coach was still miles away, when the gig and Black Beauty made their halt at the next village inn; but after long waiting a cloud of dust came in sight,—then the four grey horses, and men's hats on the top of the coach. Now Ted had made Black Beauty stand full in view across the road, while he concealed himself behind the gig.

"There's father!" said William, and standing up he seemed ready to spring from the top of the coach, before ever it stopped at the Inn. And then in a minute more, he added, "Why, Joe, I declare, if there isn't Black Beauty waiting for some one! how unfortunate, just when father's come!"

"Oh, father's got all over that now," said Joe, "and does not mind the sight of him the least!"

William looked at Joe as if he doubted not only the fact, but also that Joe could suppose forgetfulness possible; but he said nothing, and the coach stopped, and William was the first to set foot on the ground, and he wrung his father's hand with a grasp that said more than words; and then—quite unable to resist the temptation, turned to speak to Black Beauty. The faithful creature knew his young master, and had chafed and stamped after William's descent from the coach till he turned and laid his hand upon his neck.

"Why, Ted, my boy, what are you doing here?" said William, suddenly perceiving his younger brother.

"Holding your horse for you, sir."

"O Ted, Ted!" said William, half-reproachfully; "do you know who the horse is waiting for?"

"For you, sir!"

"Come, come!" said William, "no joking about that! Now, father, if Joe has the luggage, we'll be off."

Joe had been engaged in securing the packages William seemed to have forgotten, and then stepping to Black Beauty's side, Joe took the bridle from Ted, and putting it in William's hand, said, "Your merchant-brother, William, has bought him back—the first-fruits of his earnings."

"You don't mean it?" said William.

"Yes, Will, but I do; and none can say he is the worse for being twice bought and sold for the sake of a brother!" William looked on Joe—and that look was enough, but still he said in a low tone, "O Joe, I little thought of this, when you were so bent on saving!" And he sprang on Black Beauty, who knew his rider, and gently rearing, darted forward, on—by the well-known lanes, past the old familiar fields where every tree and hedge-row seemed to greet his return; on—out of sight and sound of the tardier steed behind him, swiftly on, his own horse bore him, to the home of his heart and toil! There in the sweet summer evening, his mother stood and watched with Rose, not on the door-step. but beside the garden-gate; while Rover at the first cadence of Black Beauty's measured trot, bounded down the sloping greensward, and hearing his master's greeting whistle, tried once and again to leap upon his horse, and welcome him there. But on Black Beauty bore his rider—till he sprang from the saddle to meet his mother's kiss and tear of welcome, and fold his sister to his heart; while the horse stood unheld beside him, looking on—as if with sympathising feelings.

It was finally decided by force of William's and Joe's persuasions, that as there was yet a fortnight at least before harvest, farmer and Mrs. Smith should accompany Joe and Ted on their return to London, to have the satisfaction of seeing Ted's captain and ship, and for their own refreshment and interest: while William and Rose kept all in order at home. So they went up accordingly, Ted in high spirits at the prospect before him, with William's full approval at the attainments he had made; and neither father nor mother harassed by any home anxieties to lessen the pleasure of their visit. The novelty of the complete change was very beneficial to both farmer and Mrs. Smith. They were most kindly entertained by their children's friends; the old merchant receiving them at his country-house to dinner, and promising Mrs. Smith the first opportunity that offered to come down and spend a day or two at the farm; adding that he should take care to bring her son Joseph with him, for he was quite sure he was a son that never went down to his home without a welcome for himself and all he took with him! Mrs. Smith confessed that London was not so bad as she expected, and might do very well for people not used to the country! Joe insisted on paying all the expense of the visit, which he said was a pleasure his labour had earned—and that now having bought Black Beauty, had his parents in London, and obtained a place on shipboard for Ted—he should begin life again with fresh spirit. Ted was left with Joe and Samson, ready to take his place on board ship as soon as necessary; and farmer and Mrs. Smith returned, greatly refreshed and benefitted by the inspiriting change.

On the evening of the day of their return, William asked his father and mother to take a walk across the farm with him and Rose, to which they agreed; William with gravest composure, walked and talked at their side; but Rose seemed to find it difficult to keep their meditative pace; she was always before them, leading the way, till at last they came in sight of the two white cottages with gardens stretching at either end, built by farmer Smith's mother, and lost by him through means of the only loan he ever borrowed. Rose still led the way, till her parents had nearly reached them, then turning round, she looked all expectation at William.

"O you secret keeper!" said he, "you tell it twenty times over! I shall know how to trust you again!"

"Why, Will, I never said a word!" replied Rose, coming to his side.

"No, nor much need you should!" he answered, smiling. And then turning to his father he said, "There, father, it was grandmother's cottages kept me this last year in London!"

"Your grandmother's cottages! What do you mean?"

"Because, father, when I went away from home, I came the last thing and looked at them, and I resolved I never would leave business in London if I could help it, till I had bought them back for you! I got put from it twice, with getting Joe up and Samson, but I kept on at my aim. Joe and I shared one room as we did at home, and no one would have believed, perhaps, for how little we managed; but I found last year the man had no mind to part with them, and I was forced to offer a higher sum than I had by me, so the purchase was fixed for this year—and I stayed on to earn it. And now, mother, if farming quite fails, there's a cottage rent-free for you and father and Rose, and another beside it for me—and my hands will be able, I should hope, with God's blessing, to earn bread for us all! They are bought in father's name, and are as much his as they ever were. I knew that was the best sheaf I could reap and bring home for him and for you!"

This was true—no earthly gift could perhaps have so much gratified farmer Smith. His mother's cottages, left to him by will, lost by debt, and now restored by his son—effacing the memory of the loss to him so painful, were a treasured possession indeed!

"There's a refuge then, at least, now, mother!" said William, as his mother turned silently to take his arm home.

"Yes, Will, my son's refuge for me on Earth: and, I trust, my Saviour's in Heaven!"

So William returned to his home, and began life as a farmer again.

XII.

Jem's Wedding-Day.

"God setteth the solitary in families."—Psalm, lxviii. 6.
"For with the same measure that ye mete withal, it shall be measured to you again."—Luke, vi. 38.

THE sun rose bright one summer morning, over the misty village, over the Hall with its long verdant slopes and spreading woods, over the farm with its barns and stacks and sleeping cattle, over the lonely cottage of Jem—where fruitfulness and luxuriance in trees, vegetables, and flowers, bore witness to "the hand of the diligent which maketh rich." The village was still asleep, but Jem was in his garden, "tighting it up," as he called it, though all looked tight enough, and neither leaf nor petal, tree or flower, seemed there, on that bright morning, to show one trace of Earth's decay. Jem was not watching the sun to tell the time at which to start off to tend his sheep; this was no day of pastoral work for Jem, but a day of rest, and gladness, and blessing—it was the wedding-day of honest faithful Jem. Nearly two years he had held his new abode; his mother grew more feeble with advancing age, and Jem thought to add comfort to her life, as well as to his own, by the event of that day. So thought Jem's aged mother also; and when the sun sent his first golden beam through her lattice-window on that bright morning, she had already left her pillow, and was preparing to put all things "straight" within doors: and all the while she stirred about with her best strength, she said within herself, "How tight and clean SHE will keep all when she takes charge! I know she will, and comfort me up too, and learn me a deal more of Heavenly things than I can come at now!"

At the Hall, Mercy was up before the lark had risen to chant his first glad song at Heaven's gate, and now she hastened down the misty road with her bridesmaid's attire in a handkerchief on her arm, to help her grandmother put all things straight, and then to hasten on to stand beside the bride.

Mrs. Smith might have been up since midnight—for all the sun could tell when he first looked across the farm, and glanced in radiance through its uncurtained window-panes. Rose was moving, working, speaking, as quick again as usual—as if all the labour of that day had to be completed before the day had well begun, Farmer Smith was out in the freshening morning air, giving directions to his men; and William was helping the yard-boy sweep the garden-walks, and the path down the sloping greensward. And where was Patience—the faithful servant always at hand when work was to be done, the faithful servant through years of trial, sorrow, peace,—where was Patience?—Kneeling alone in her chamber, looking up through its small window to the rosy sky above her head, thinking on the past, the present, and the future, till tears overflowed her eyes, and she hid her face and wept; then enshrining all her thoughts and feelings in one fervent thanksgiving and prayer, she went down to the family below:—This was her wedding-day, and she the affianced bride of Jem.

"There now, child, we don't want you standing about in the way!" exclaimed Mrs. Smith, as she saw Patience looking on, at a loss how to act without being told. "Go and be after anything you may want to get done," added Mrs. Smith. So Patience had her time to herself. Rose at last went to put on her bridesmaid's dress; and Mercy came down to the farm in hers—and she dressed the bride; and William put on his Sunday suit, he was to walk by the side of the bride and give her away in the Church—for she had no relative on Earth to stand beside her there. But before they set out, Mrs. Smith said to Patience alone, "Patience, girl, I know they say black should should never be worn at a wedding! but you won't be against my wearing that black silk, as I always do on Sundays, for the sake of little Tim? Not but what I know his robes are as white as the driven snow, but I did not like for myself any other colour in silk, and being for him—it could not tell of an evil to come! I know you won't mind, but I thought I would just name it beforehand." Patience answered with a tear; for she too had been thinking of the child, and how he had been her little comforter there, and how he loved Jem! and she could not help wishing he could be with them then, though she knew it was better to have entered Heaven — safe from all changes, and sorrow, and sin.

Widow Jones did not go to the Church; nor would she consent to lock up the cottage and come to the wedding-feast at the farm. She said she was wanted "to keep things straight at home;" whether she knew some mischievous spider to be lurking in some hole or corner, all ready to disfigure the pattern of neatness she had finished off within; or whether she wished to be there to give Jem and his bride her motherly greeting at the threshold of their home, she did not say; the only reason she gave was the "keeping things straight," and this one word "straight" with widow Jones admitted a meaning so full, and application so endless, that it often might baffle the learning of most to discover the precise point she had in view under this word of a use universal! And it proved well that widow Jones did keep her resolve to "bide in the house," for reasons far more important than keeping dust or spiders at a distance, with apron or broom.

A trusty man and boy were in waiting at the farm, and no sooner was the bridal-party off for the Church, than Mrs. Smith said to her husband, "Now, don't lose a minute, for things are quicker done than you would think for, and they will be back in no time!" So saying, Mrs. Smith hastened off with farmer Smith and the trusty man and boy to the farther barn, where the wedding-gifts had been placed in readiness by William that morning. Mrs. Smith looked upon them with fresh satisfaction. She had said, "The girl has served me like a child, and she shall not be sent away like a stranger!" And no one who looked into the barn that morning could doubt Mrs. Smith having kept her resolve. First stood the gift of her mistress to Patience, the prettiest of young heifers, as black as a raven's wing, with one star of white on its broad forehead. Rose had named it "Black Beauty," after the favourite horse. Mrs. Smith said, that, as a bit of meadow-land went with the cottage, there could be no reason why Patience should not have a cow of her own, and sell milk to the poor! which was a thing, Mrs. Smith said, that wanted to be done more than it was; she was thankful that for her part she could say, that never, with her knowledge, had the poor been sent away with an empty can, when they came up to buy a little milk for their families, if she had any in the dairy to supply them. Mrs. Smith knew how to give generously when she did give, and beside the young heifer, stood a new milk-pail, two milk-pans, a cream-pot and skimmer; all these were the wedding-gifts of her mistress to Patience. But then Patience had been no common servant—the nurse and comforter of little Tim, her mistress's own devoted nurse, when infection and death were near, and in her service faithful in all things—this Patience had been, and her mistress was resolved to testify her sense of it. Next stood the gift of Rose to Patience,—a pair of hens of perfect whiteness, with a black cock, all reared on the farm. The fowls were in a basket, chiefly constructed by the hands of the sailor-boy, his mother bestowed it on Patience, having another of a different kind herself; for she said, that to leave her sailor-boy out, would look as if he were no longer one of themselves! In a corner of the barn a little black pig was enclosed, waiting for his removal to fresh quarters—this was farmer Smith's gift to his servant Jem. Added to these was a new barrow, made at the village wheelwright's, a famous substitute for the one that Jem had used from a child—and which the largest nails would now hardly avail to hold together, this was William's present to his favourite farm-servant. But these were not all; Mrs. Smith had a maxim which she often used, applying it variously as occasion served, and this was the maxim, "There's no good in remembering one to forget another!" Accordingly Mrs. Smith said she was not going to overlook Jem, as if she had altogether forgotten the value to be set by his services. What she had saved by his care in eggs and young fowls when he was yard-boy, she said she knew pretty well by the loss when his master took him away to make him a shepherd—she had never been able to get up, or keep, such a poultry-yard since! But Jem should see his mistress had not forgotten him! And there, in demonstration of the fact, stood a small box containing household linen, bleached and made by Mrs. Smith. In this same box was a shawl from Samson, chosen and bought by him in his uncle's shop, and sent down from London for Patience. While, from all the great city could offer, Joe had chosen for Jem an engraving of the Good Shepherd, with the sheep gathered near Him, when he said to Peter, "Feed my Lambs;" framed with a glass before it, Joe sent it down to gleam from the cottage walls of the village shepherd, with its light of holy and blessed remembrance.

No sooner did Mrs. Smith with hasty step arrive at the barn, than the whole array of gifts began to receive their dismissal Farmer Smith haltered the young heifer and led her himself; while a tumbril received all the rest, as nicely adjusted as the case admitted of—the boy down in the midst securing he little black pig, the box in the barrow, and the fowls on the top of the box, while the milk-pail with its bright rims, the dairy pans, cream-pot and skimmer, were all settled in, and the tumbril drove off.

Farmer Smith arrived first with the young black heifer. Widow Jones in the midst of her business within, was still looking from time to time from the window, to see what might be happening without. And now she saw farmer Smith at the stile with the heifer. "Why, if there isn't our master himself, and that handsome black heifer!" said widow Jones with surprise; and making haste from the door, she got down to the moveable stile just as farmer Smith had lifted it out to lead in the heifer. "Well, neighbour," said kind farmer Smith, in his most cheerful tone, —which tone always rose up when his words had to do with gifts or any token of good will,— "Well, neighbour, I am sure I wish you joy to-day; though you will just please to remember that you are growing rich by making us poorer! I don't mean because the black heifer is to stay as yours, instead of ours—no, I don't mean it of anything money could have bought—but of her who's your daughter by this time, if the Minister kept to his hour at the church! I made her servant-girl to my wife, who must choose for herself now—for I am sure I can't hope to please her so well any more!" Widow Jones stood in silent surprise. The black heifer for them! Could it possibly be, that farmer Smith had led down the handsomest of all his young heifers for her children! "Come, then," said farmer Smith, "there are plenty more things on the way, let's make one safe at a time. You tell Patience, her mistress has sent her the heifer, with her love and her blessing; and there's a milk-pail and pans, and a cream-pot and skimmer, that Patience may sell milk to the poor; for it's a fact in this village, that the poor often don't know how to get half a pint, and I wish that some one would name it to the Squire, that he might just speak to his tenants about it!" O with what wondering eyes of delight and of joy poor old widow Jones looked on, while her master, as she always called farmer Smith, led up the black heifer and made her fast in the warmly-thatched shed! But there was no time allowed for expressing her feeling; farmer Smith hastened back to the stile where the tumbril was waiting, and widow Jones hastened after, and she stood by while its stores were unloaded. Out tumbled the little black pig, and the boy jumped down just in time to secure him: then came the milk-pail and milk-pans, the cream-pot and the skimmer;

the box tied round with a cord and directed; the handsome white and black fowls; and, last of all, the new barrow for Jem. Farmer Smith gave the messages one by one to widow Jones, who stood listening beside him in the midst of the things; there she stood in her short-sleeved, half-length, large flowered, print gown, bought new for the wedding occasion, and put on first by her that day, her snow-white kerchief beneath it with its thick folds in front, and her single-crimped bordered cap, with a scarlet ribbon pinned round it—saving all need of strings, and her white apron tied on, all ready for whatever on that summer-day might befall; there she stood wiping away with the corner of her apron her fast-starting tears, as she listened to farmer Smith and looked on the gifts—all telling the praises, so sweet to her, of her Jem and his bride! "The box," said farmer Smith, "will speak for itself when it's opened, which need not be done till your children return. The fowls are from Rose, her present to Patience; my wife says Patience will know who made the basket, and she is to keep it for our poor sailor-boy's sake. My son William had the barrow made on purpose for Jem; he says Jem is not to think too much about him in the gift, for he had it made as much in remembrance of our poor little Tim, who always took such a fancy to Jem; my son had a wish that Jem should have something to serve him through life, in remembrance of the child. But I must be off, for my wife set her mind on my being back and knowing the things safe here, before they returned from the Church." So farmer Smith saw the little black pig secure in the stye; and then leaving the man and boy to help in with the rest, he hastened back again to the farm.

Mrs. Smith was impatiently waiting her husband's return, and losing more time by her looks from the window and door than she gained by her haste in all things beside. But now seeing him ascending the hill she was satisfied; she heard of the safe bestowment of all, the messages delivered as she had given them in charge; and then bringing out farmer Smith's Sunday coat, she waited in something more like quiet expectation for the bridal party's return from the church.

And now in the distance the party came in sight. Jem led his bride, Rose and Mercy followed after, and William beside them. Mrs. Smith gave one hasty glance into her parlour to be assured all was right there, then hurried to the door-step to receive them. Farmer Smith held open the small garden-gate, and gave them his hand, and blessed them as they entered; then smiled on Rose and Mercy, and shut the gate after them all. There stood Mrs. Smith, in her Sunday gown of black silk, upright on the door-step; but when Jem led up his bride, she stooped her tall figure, and kissed the cheek of Patience, and led her in herself, as with a mother's feeling. The water was boiling, so the tea was soon made, the coffee was ready beforehand; and full of gentlest cheerfulness they all sat down to the wedding-breakfast. Mrs. Smith poured out the tea and Rose the coffee; Jem and his bride sat on one side of the table; and Mercy between farmer Smith and William on the other. No pains had been spared in preparing the feast; a plum-cake, black with richness, was placed in the centre; it was not frosted over with snow, which the art of the confectioners alone can accomplish—such borrowed skill was not needed at this wedding-feast, nor would Mrs. Smith have seen the merit of crusting a cake with a coating of ice, for a table round which only affection could gather. Ornaments they had—nature's own, and not wanting in taste of arrangement. Rose had gathered white lilies, and laid them over and in a circle round the cake which her mother had made; and strewn on the white table-cloth, in long winding lines, lay the flowers of the season reposing; while round the plate of the bridegroom and bride bloomed a circle of nothing but heart's-ease. Among the frail flowers stood the solid mass of the dishes—a great pie filled with rabbits, a ham dressed for the occasion, a fresh-cut cheese from the dairy, with butter made into swans that floated in a lake of water or reposed on green borders of parsley. Each corner dish was a large shining loaf, with a circle of smallest loaves in the plate round it. Cakes of every description—all home-made, with fruits from the garden; sweet wine in glass decanters; and a tankard for ale. While the faces around looked down on those smiling flowers, and the fingers of tenderest care still on all sides removed them—when any change of the dishes might have pressed on their forms; for the recklessness that can gather together the fairest flowers of the Earth, to please the eyes of those who will take no care to preserve their Heaven-given loveliness, is not found in the poor man's home, nor in the dwellings of those who sow and reap the ground

Meanwhile, at the cottage, widow Jones had scarcely marked the progress of time, intent on the interest of her newly-arrived charge. "Pretty creatures!" said widow Jones, "sure enough I must find them some food!" So stooping down her aged figure, she cut up some grass and mixed it with such leaves as a cow, she well knew would like, and then strewed it before the black heifer, who licked the old woman's hand before feeding, as she used to do the hand of Patience—who had brought her up from a calf; then, having no corn of any description, widow Jones crumbled up a small piece of bread for the fowls, though she said as she showered it over them, that it would have been a shame on any other day to give them such food! And finally she cut up a few vegetables for the pig. The creatures all liking their food, and the notice bestowed on them in their strange quarters, called after the dear old woman, till she heard such a lowing and cackling and grunting, that she hastened back to see after them again; but at last, quite fatigued, she told them all, gravely, that they must think she had something else to do than to see after them! and having ventured so far in a reproof for their persevering demands, she returned to the house, and putting the small kettle on the little back-kitchen fire, made herself a quiet cup of tea, which greatly refreshed her,—so much so, that after the toil and excitement of the morning she fell asleep in her arm-chair. She slept quietly there for some half-hour or more, when a sudden sharp rap at the door aroused her. "They are come!" thought widow Jones, as she started up from sleep; but no, it was not her son who opened the door, and looked in, it was a stranger. "Is this Roodes' plot?" asked the man. "Yes," replied widow Jones, rather in alarm at sight of the stranger. "I suppose you are the mother of the man who lives here?" "Yes," said widow Jones, still more uneasy. "Then you will please to give your son that letter, from Madam Clifford at the Hall, and be so good as to show us where to set up this eight-day clock!" Widow Jones looked out, and there at the stile stood a light cart, with another man in it, and the eight-day clock! But before she had time time to consider, the men were in with the clock, and soon fixed on the best place to put it in themselves, and, finding the old woman had no objection to their choice of situation, they set it up at once, observing as they did so, that it was one of the best time-keepers ever put together; and before widow Jones had recovered enough from her surprise to do more than look at the outside of the letter in her hand, from that to the clock, and then back again to the sealed letter, the men were gone, and the cart, and all out of sight like a dream—except that there stood the clock, ticking each moment of time, and over the bright hands at the top of its face, a coloured picture of a shepherd-lad with a lamb on one arm, and his sheep feeding at his feet. It was well widow Jones had had her cup of tea and her refreshing sleep, for most surely neither would have been thought of after the arrival of the clock. "Then it's from Madam herself, for my Jem on his wedding-day!" at last said widow Jones, as she once more looked at the letter. "Well!" she added, "if all this is not wonderful, I don't know what is!" and lifting a thankful look upward, old widow Jones sat down again in her arm-chair, to consider all things over before her children's arrival.

When Patience at the farm at last turned to take leave, Mrs Smith's pleasant smile was gone, her lip quivered, and her strong firm voice faltered. Patience could not tell her own feeling in words, but none needed to hear it spoken, her years of faithful service left no doubt of that. The moment passed, and the maid and her mistress had parted, the record of her years in that place of service was finished, and nothing of the past could be altered. How often does that solemn moment come and go unheeded—a service is ended, a place left, and the past is supposed to be done with; but the record of that past—what is written there? that moment of parting has sealed it, and it lies from that time in the hand of the Judge, until the day, that will bring all secret things to light, must see it unfolded. In the hands of the Judge lie the records of the past years of all; and not one created being can unfold or read them, still less alter a single word they contain. But there is One, and only One, to whom they still lie open—even Jesus the Saviour of sinners; and earnest prayer to Him may still avail to get all the hand-writing against us blotted out in His blood; only let us not go thoughtlessly forward—as if those records of the past contained no sentence against us! For Patience the record was blessed; and she knew the secret of Prayer to that Saviour, whose blood cleanseth from all sin

—blotting out all His people's transgressions, and making their imperfections perfect. So Patience had parted in peace, beneath the blessing of Heaven and of Earth, and was now descending the hill. Mrs. Smith waited a few moments, looking out of the window, in the effort to recover composure; then turning to Rose, who was watching beside her, she said, "I wish you would run after Patience with that," taking a book done up in paper from her pocket, "you know what it is, I did not feel able to speak about it when she went, as I meant to have done. You can tell her it's for the sake of little Tim!" Rose took the book, and her swift steps soon overtook Patience, who, leaning on Jem, was ascending the opposite hill. "Patience, mother sends you this, it's a book of family prayer, like the one my aunt gave her; she wishes you to keep it for the sake of little Tim; she meant to have given it to you herself, only she was so overcome at your going!" Patience took the small parcel, and looking back at the farm, sent a message by Rose of her duty and her thanks to her mistress, with the assurance that they would take it into use every day.

Mercy stayed at the farm to assist Mrs. Smith and Rose, in the clearing away; and to make things more cheerful there where she was a favourite with all. And now at length widow Jones, looking out from above the bright geraniums in

JEM'S WEDDING DAY.

Ministering Children. Vol. II, p 246

the window, saw Jem and his bride at the stile. Then she opened wide the cottage-door, and stood just within—while the sheltering vine one side, and the drooping honeysuckle on the other, softly shaded the view of her now feeble figure. Patience walked up the path first, and Jem followed close after, and the old woman stretched out both her arms and clasped them round Patience, and Patience threw hers round the old woman's neck, and felt for the first time in life, that she too had a mother! Then as Patience unlocked that close embrace, the old woman turning to her son said, "God bless you, my Jem, and bless us all here together, for I am sure 'tis His goodness that brings such things to pass!" and Jem looked on as if he felt the sight he then saw was the best sight of all. But just then, Jem started and stared, for a loud striking clock told the hour, with a slow decided call upon the attention of all.

"Why, mother! a clock! where did it come from?"

"Ah! never mind that!" replied widow Jones, "look here in this drawer, here's a letter in Madam Clifford's own hand—if that don't tell you all about it, I am sure that I can't!"

Jem took up the letter.

"But now, child, come, sit down," said the old woman, turning to Patience. "Why, to think that you have never been inside the door, and yet all these months you have known the place was just waiting for you!"

Jem had opened the letter, but finding it not easy to read in a moment of time, he folded it up for a better opportunity, and turned again to his bride, and then leaning on the back of her chair, told his aged mother, who was seated before him, of the feast their good mistress had made at the farm; while Patience held closely that treasured book of prayer, and looked round on her new abode. What comfort beamed upon her from every corner; and there lay the large Bible, dear old Willy's own Bible, of which Jem had so often told her! She longed to look on its pages where the old man had read, but she said nothing then; and Jem seemed to wish to give her time to look round: and poor old widow Jones looked so happy on the two, that she seemed in no hurry either to move or to speak.

"Well," at last Jem asked with his own cheerful smile, "Do you think it looks anything like what you fancied, and as if you could content yourself here?"

"Not like what I fancied!" said Patience, looking up, "you never told me how beautiful it was inside; I never saw such a home as it is for any like us!"

"Ah, that was all our young Squire's doing!" said Jem, "and I don't know, but somehow a blessing seems to bide with it all, for it always looks as beautiful and cheerful as can be, just as you see it looks now!"

"But what a clock that is!" said Patience, "do you see that shepherd with the lamb in his arms? and the clock is so like ours at the farm, it seems quite natural to look at it!"

"Yes," replied Jem, "I never was more taken by surprise in my life than when it set up striking just as we had come in at the door! it seemed as if it must have a word to say to us also! but I don't seem to have thought about it yet. I can't think," added Jem, "what that kind of grunting is I hear, I could almost have thought my poor little pig that I lost had come to life again, to welcome you here!"

Then old widow Jones rose up from her chair, and said, "I advise you to go and see what it is, and settle your mind about it at once!" So Jem opened the door into the back-kitchen, when a loud shrill crow from a cock burst on the ear of Patience.

"You come and all!" said Jem to Patience, who hastened after him, the aged mother following—to the pig-stye; there looked up the little black pig, grunting eagerly again as if quite sure now of a feast; and then turning away from Jem and Patience, looked up at widow Jones, as she, his kind feeder, arrived at the stye.

"Why, mother, what a beauty of a pig!" exclaimed Jem, "however in the world did you get it? Why, it's just like one of master's at the farm!"

"I am not going to tell you everything in a moment!" said widow Jones, decidedly; while the cock, at the sound of pleasant voices, crowed forth a further announcement of his presence on the premises. Jem stepped on to the shed and opened the door, then holding it back, said in amaze, "Patience, only you look in here!" Patience looked in; there stood the black heifer, who at sight of Patience pulled hard at the rope, by which she was tied, to get to her side; there stood the new barrow; the hens and the cock—in the basket made by the sailor-boy Ted. "Now, you just listen," said widow Jones, "and I'll tell you all!" So Jem stood there and listened, still all in amaze, and Patience beside him—while the black heifer was happy with her hand which it licked on both sides.

"I was here in the house then," said widow Jones, "keeping all straight within; when, who should I see but our master leading up the young heifer! Out I went; and he told me he had brought it from our mistress, a present for Patience—for her very own, and he said she was to have it and sell milk to the poor: and it seemed to me wholly a beautiful thing, that she who had been altogether a comfort up there, should come here to a home and sell milk to the poor! But that was just what our master said; and if you will believe, there's the whole concern for the milking come too! It's all set out in the dairy; just you come and look." Back widow Jones hurried, and Patience and Jem followed after, to see the milk-pail with its bright rims, the milk-pans, and cream-pot and skimmer, all set out in the dairy. Then, turning again, widow Jones went on to tell all the history, not shortened the least by her remarks in between the matters of fact that she had to relate; how the fowls were from Rose; the basket the sailor-boy's work, and all that their master had said about it; and the barrow for Jem, to serve him for life, in remembrance of the love of little Tim. Then followed the box and all its contents—quite new to widow Jones; the house-linen, the shawl, and the picture; till Patience could bear up no longer against such tokens of affection and kindness, and tying on her bonnet, she said, "I tell you what, Jem, before ever we do anything more I must go down to the farm, and you with me, and speak about what we found here!" So Patience and Jem returned again to the farm, and going in by the back-door, found Mrs. Smith still busy clearing away; Patience sat down in the low-backed kitchen chair, where she sat in tears the day little Tim first took notice of her; she could not now speak a word, but, quite overcome, she hid her face and wept, while Jem stood silent beside her. "Why, Patience, child!" said Mrs. Smith, stopping short with a cloth in her hand with which she was rubbing up the tankard; "come back so soon! why, child, what's the matter?"

"It's only your goodness, and master's too," sain Jem; "indeed it's all over too much for us both!"

"Well now, if that's all," replied Mrs. Smith, "you have done and said quite enough, so never let me hear another word about that, nor your master either—here he is close by to say the same."

"But the black heifer!" said Patience without looking up; "I am sure I never could have thought it! I thought I was leaving all the creatures behind, and then, when I got up there—why they seemed all up there before me!"

"And where could they have been better, child, I should like to know?" replied Mrs. Smith. "Haven't you and Jem just tended them all with that care that nothing seemed to be lost that was under your hand? You know that very well; and though it's just what every one who has a right principle would do, yet I was not going to seem as if I did not know it, for I did, and your master no less! And I do say, if there's one in the village who has more of a right than another to sell milk for the poor, it's just you and Jem! I know I have always taken a pleasure in that, and I am pretty sure you will no less; and such a fancy as we all had for the black heifer—what could we wish better for her than to live for serving the poor with her milk! Why I am sure I little thought you would not get over the day without being down here again! But it's just your way for all that, and you may be sure I shall soon come up and look after you; so not a word more about anything—you remember I have said it!" And with that Mrs. Smith made an end of her reply.

And now in looked Rose and Mercy, both ready for a walk, all surprise at sight of Patience and Jem.

"Why, here's Rose and Mercy coming off up to you, and you not at home to receive them! There now, be satisfied, and don't shed another tear over that which comes only as a blessing!" said Mrs. Smith; and then adding, "Good-bye to you, my good girl, I don't think any the worse of you for coming so quick down!" and with fresh and livelier parting words than before, Patience again hastened back to her cottage-home with Jem.

The good mother had set out the tea all in readiness—the picture of comfort. Rose and Mercy followed after. Rose bearing the round wedding-cake, and Mercy carrying all the white lilies in an open farm-basket on her arm, and a nosegay of the flowers in her hand. The cake was set down in the middle of the table, and Rose would do and look at nothing till she had covered it again with its lilies—to the admiration of widow Jones. After visiting all the creatures with Patience and Mercy and Jem, Rose hastened back again to the farm; while Jem and his bride, and his mother and Mercy sat down at the round cottage-table. Then Mrs. Clifford's letter was brought out again: and Mercy knew her mistress's hand-writing, and was able to read it every word to the pleasure of the whole party.

Now Jem began to consider how he could get his duty and his thanks to Madam Clifford; he consulted with Mercy whether she thought he might make bold and step up that evening and ask to speak to the young Squire; or whether he ought to wait till the next day. Jem's grateful heart did not like to pass the day over without offering his thanks; he was dressed also in his best, which seemed suitable for going up to the Hall on such an occasion; but still more than this, Jem had a feeling of not liking to pass his wedding-day over without so much as a sight of the young Squire:—he seemed to think that all could not go so well with him if he went over the day without a sight of him; so it was decided that after tea he should walk up. But while they were still seated round at the table, the cottage-door wide open, in that summer afternoon, and Jem seated in full view of the road, he suddenly started up, saying, "There's our young Squire himself at the stile!" So Jem hastened out; there Herbert stood, with a noble dog waiting beside him. "Well, Jem," said the young Squire, "I could not be the only one not to wish you well in a friendly greeting to-day, so I walked down this way, expecting now I should find you at home." Then Jem sent his best message of duty and gratitude to Madam Clifford for the handsomest clock, Jem said, he ever had seen! And he asked the young Squire if he would please to walk in and see how it stood. Herbert went in with Jem, and there he saw that dwelling of comfort and peace; the tall clock with the shepherd-lad and the young lamb on his arm painted on it; the lily-covered cake; the aged mother in her new array; and Patience and Mercy beside her. The young Squire sat down, and the dog sat at his feet and looked up in his face. Then Herbert said, "Jem, now you are a rich man, and I thought you might manage to keep a good dog. I had this from some distance for you, one of the best of his kind, I believe; he is a huge fellow, but he won't cost you more, I fancy, than you will be willing to spend on him. What do you say to having him for a helper?"

"Well, sir," replied Jem, "to my thinking, he looks to have sense enough to keep sheep by himself!"

At Jem's wit they all laughed, and the young Squire was quite satisfied; but he said, "You must take a little notice of him at first, or I am afraid he will run off to me, for I have made a great favourite of him; we must tie him up for to night. And see here, I have brought a cord, for I remembered that you only engaged for a pair of hands—when I came to you supposing you furnished with ropes for drawing up the log from the ditch!" The young Squire went with Jem to fasten up the dog, and then Jem showed him the presents received that day; and to be able to show them to him seemed to double the joy Jem felt in them all; and if the black heifer was a treasure to Patience, what was not the noble shepherd's dog to Jem—the young Squire's own gift! Then the Squire heard how Patience was to sell milk to the poor, and this led him to inquire why there should be occasion for that; and then he found from Jem that all the farmers made their milk into cheese, and so had none to sell, except farmer Smith; and the Squire made a note in his book of the fact, and remembered it in years to come. Then he left honest Jem with his bride and his mother in old Willy's cottage—and returned to the Hall.

After tea, while Patience and Mercy cleared away, Jem went after food for the creatures; he longed to take his dog with him, but he could not venture so soon. Then the sun went down in the sky; and when all the live creatures were provided for, before Mercy returned to the Hall, Jem opened old Willy's Bible, and while they all sat round, he read the 103d Psalm, and then they knelt down, and he offered up the evening prayer from the book Mrs. Smith had given in remembrance of little Tim. And so closed that bright summer's day.

XIII.

Conclusion.

"When the ear heard, then it blessed me; and when the eye saw, it gave witness to me: because I delivered the poor that cried, and the fatherless, and him that had none to help him. The blessing of him that was ready to perish came upon me: and I caused the widow's heart to sing for joy."—Job. xxix. 11-13.

SOON after the young Squire came of age, it was necessary to appoint a fresh steward for the estate on which he resided, to watch over and receive the rents of the farms, and for all such affairs as belong to the office of a farm-steward. He had looked forward to this change, and made his own choice as to who should fill this office—so important in the manner of its exercise to the comfort as well as to the integrity of those over whom the steward was appointed to watch. No sooner was the office vacant than William was sent for to the Hall, and it was offered to him. Farmer Smith's farm was not large, and it would be easy for William still to live with his parents, assist his father on the farm, and yet accomplish all that this new employment would require of him; while the yearly salary received, would make the circumstances of his family all he could desire—for it was only the difficulty of always being ready with his rent that kept farmer Smith's mind harassed by his business. So William gratefully accepted the offer, and was appointed farm-steward of the estate.

A year passed peacefully over Patience in her new abode; and when the summer came again—with its long days and refreshing fruits, she received a visit from her first master's family; they came over to spend a day, to the joy of all, —but especially of Esther, who was left for a month's visit with Patience, till she became so fond of all country sights and sounds—of the black cow with its brimming pail of white-frothed milk; the poor women and children coming to buy of Patience; the white hens, and little chickens who flew upon her shoulders; the shepherd's dog and the sheep; and even of feeding the pig with all that Patience put by in a plate for its food,—that she returned to her home in the town, fully resolved on being a farm-house servant, and living some day with Mrs. Smith.

Mrs. Smith had had a trying year with servants; three times in the course of the year she had been obliged to make a change; she tried to be patient, and not to expect too much, but it was all of no use; she said, she found all the servant girls of one mind—and that was idleness and finery, instead of real honest work! So thoughtless girls came and left a situation, where Patience had stayed to earn the favor of all. Mrs. Smith was quite in despair, and said she saw no help for it but doing the work herself with Rose, for such servants were more trial than all their service was worth. Patience often came down to the farm on baking-days, or churning-days, or washing-days, and stayed for some hours to help; and these were pleasant times both to her mistress and herself. One day while Patience was busy taking out the bread from the large brick oven at the farm, Mrs. Smith being then without a servant, a pleasant-looking woman came up to the door, and asked if Mrs. Smith were within.

"Yes," said Patience, and she went to let her mistress know.

"I daresay it's only a girl after the place!" said Mrs. Smith.

"No, she looks over age to be after that," replied Patience. So Mrs. Smith came down to the back-kitchen where the woman waited. Mrs. Smith looked at her for a moment as she stood there before her, then exclaimed, "Why, Molly! is it you?"

"Yes, that it is!" replied Molly, "I heard you were unsettled, and I thought perhaps you would not be against my coming back to you again, for I have never made a home in any place since I left you; and I think if I could but get back here, I should feel settled again. I am sure I have often repented that I gave up as I did instead of trying on a little longer, but I hope I should be wiser for the future!"

"Well, Molly!" said Mrs. Smith, "I always felt I was to blame for your leaving; but I hope things are better now in some respects, than they were; though the child is gone!—you know that, I suppose?"

"Yes," replied Molly, "I vexed sadly for him; it cut me up more than anything to have left him: but I hope it was all for the best for him, by what I heard."

"Well, Molly, I know you, and you know the place, and if your mind is to come back, I am sure my mind is the same, and your master's I can answer for as well as my own, and therefore there's no need to say any more words about it." So Molly came back to the farm, a more patient servant, to find a more patient mistress; and comfort was once more restored to Mrs. Smith's household arrangements.

Another pleasant event of this summer was the return of the sailor-boy from his first long voyage, full of vigor and bodily spirits. Sun-burnt, and laden with his gifts of love—he came to gladden the hearts of all; to shake heartily every friendly hand—and none were foes with him; to visit every familiar spot; to hold discourse with all the men of village-trade on the use he had made, or was likely to make, of their arts —though he had yet known no shipwreck; to learn again from the lips of the Minister—to tell him what he had seen and heard and done, and to listen to his advice for the future. He made no little stir both in the farm and village; and then, having formed a strong friendship with Jem's noble dog, comforted his mother, and satisfied his father and William, he went off again—light and swift as a bird of passage, to be tossed once more on the free crested waves.

Another year passed by, and when the next autumn came, the young Squire had completed his college life, and satisfied the best hopes of his boyhood's tutor, and it was understood in the village that he was going abroad again with his mother. These tidings gave great disappointment to the hopes of those who had looked to the comfort of his residence among them; but having assembled his tenantry, he told them that he believed his absence would not be for more than six months, and that he hoped to return and live among them for the future. He had no sooner left, than repairs and alterations were begun at the Hall; and the mansion, far from looking desolate and deserted as before, was a scene of perpetual life and activity.

Two years of unclouded comfort Patience had enjoyed in her cottage-home. Jem's aged mother, relieved from all care and toil, had regained fresh vigour and spirits—she was always busy in little ways, always at hand, always reflecting the brightness of that bright cottage-home. But the winter of the Squire's absence proved a severe one, and the cold seemed suddenly to snap the old woman's feeble stem of life, and she laid down on her bed to die! Patience could not believe, when the doctor told her that her mother's death was near. "Why, it was but a week ago," she said, "my mother was up and as cheerful and well as ever I have known her to be!" The doctor replied, "It might be so, but her hours are numbered now!" Still Patience could not believe; she thought it must be a sudden chill, and that warmth and care would restore her. She lighted and kept up, day and night, a bright little fire in the small grate up-stairs; she made cordials, and Mrs. Smith came up more than once in the day; but the old woman smiled on them and said, "It's just sweet to my old heart to feel you all bent to keep me still, if you could! but I am going where I shall be far better off even than here—though my last days have been my best days!" Then, looking up at Patience, she said, "You have just been my evening star, lighting me home—for I have gathered more knowledge these two years with you, than I had in my whole life before. Let the thought of that comfort you as long as you live! Jem, my son," she added, turning to him, "you have been your mother's staff all through the weariest of her way—which lay on this side your poor father's grave. God grant your mother's blessing may fall upon you in the hour of your need! I know you will take care of Mercy; she is not fit to stand in this rough world alone, it would soon break her down; but the God of the orphan will not let His promise fail. It is not darkness to me; the light that has but glimmered before me so long, shines all bright around me now; and I hear the voice of Him who says, "Come unto me, and I will give you rest!" So the widow departed, and her children mourned for her. Mercy was far away with Mrs. Clifford in a foreign land; but tears were shed for old widow Jones by the eyes of those who owned no tie of kindred with her. The snow lay deep upon the ground, and Patience, ill from the anxiety of nursing and the shock of so sudden a loss—having also her infant child to tend—was little fit to venture to the grave. Jem earnestly persuaded her not to go, but Patience would not be persuaded; she said it was the only respect she could now shew to one who had been all a mother could be to her; and to have lost her so suddenly—was a trial she had never so much as thought upon! Jem gave way, and Patience followed their aged mother to the grave by his side. But she took cold as might have been expected, and was soon confined to her bed. Rose now came and tended Patience and the infant, day by day, with gentlest care; and Mrs. Smith was continually contriving in every way to minister to her comfort; but, notwithstanding all this care, and Jem's ceaseless anxiety, the spring was approaching before Patience was able to leave her bed and sit down stairs in old Willy's arm-chair.

But the cheering spring advanced—the frost gave way before the sun's warm beams, the flowers raised their heads above their wintry graves, the birds looked down from tree and hedge and sang a welcome to them; new life and vigour came slowly back to Patience, and comfort to the heart of Jem. Patience had not yet milked her cow since her illness, nor stood in her dairy to help the poor people who came, nor walked down once to the farm; but the spring had set foot on the Earth, and the Earth was rejoicing at its presence, and Patience felt that her life was reviving. And now all her anxiety was to go to the Church for the Sunday's service; she said she knew when she had once been there she would seem to be well again, and able to milk her cow and attend to all her home-work. But Jem was firm now, he had sorely repented having suffered Patience to attend their mother's funeral, and he now resolved to act prudently. At length, as May was giving place to June, the very last Sunday in the month dawned as soft and lovely a day as the spring-time ever beheld. Jem could not refuse Patience her wish on such a day; so, wrapped up, and leaning on the arm of her husband, with steps more feeble than she had expected them to be, while Rose stayed with the infant in the cottage, Patience went to the afternoon service in the Church.

The Minister—their own Minister, preached a Missonary sermon; and when he told of the poor heathen without God—because without Christ, and therefore without hope in the world, Patience thought she could feel something of what it must be to live, sicken and die, without one glimpse of Heaven, one hope of entering there! She thought of her dying mother's peace, she thought of her husband's Christian life, she thought of her child baptised in her Saviour's Name, she thought of her own faith and hope—and she longed to do something for the poor heathen as a token of her thankfulness to God, and her pity for them. But what could she do? Their mother's funeral, and the doctor's long attendance on her, had taken all Jem's savings. Jem's last week's wages were all spent on the Saturday except one shilling, which he had in his pocket, and that she would not ask him for, because perhaps he might be thinking of giving it himself. If Patience had known of the collection, she would have tried to save something back for it on the Saturday; but Jem had not told her — most likely he had forgotten it himself. What could she do? Patience had still one treasure, a possession in money that she always kept with her. She had kept it through want and distress, through trouble and sickness, through prosperity and comfort: she had thought to keep it through life, and that nothing would ever win it from her—it was the Lady's half-crown, the first gift she had ever received from the hand of love; her first knowledge of tenderness was bound up with that gift; and she had kept it, as her treasured possession, through all her life's changes. But now the call to part with it entered her heart —it seemed to come from Heaven, and Earth seemed to repeat the same call—"Is it too much for you to give up, to send the Name of your Saviour to those who never heard the blessed sound of pardon and Heaven through Jesus Christ?" Patience felt the question deep within her heart, and she resolved — "No, I will part with it for that!" But now a trial of her resolution came, Jem crossed from the men's benches, after service, to her and slipped their remaining shilling into her hand, saying, "It's all we have, so you must give it!"

"No," replied Patience, "I have something besides, you must give that!" Jem looked at her, as if thinking she must be mistaken, but seeing her decided, he took the shilling, and put it himself into the plate as he passed out. Patience followed slowly, and dropped her half-crown into the same plate, then, as if in a moment, her heart seemed lightened and her steps strengthened. Her husband was waiting for her outside the door, and she walked home by his side.

The sky that Sabbath afternoon was beautiful before them as they descended the hill. When they reached their peaceful cottage the door stood partly open, and they heard the voice of Rose singing to their infant; she had reached the last verse of the "Cradle Hymn," and the parents heard her clear voice breathing their hearts' desire and hers over the infant sleeping in her arms,—

> "May'st thou live to know and fear Him,
> Trust and love Him all thy days;
> Then go dwell for ever near Him,
> See His face and sing His praise!"

The father and mother entered their cottage; the kettle was boiling on the wood-fire, the tea was set ready on the round table, and all looked the picture of repose. Rose hastened back to the farm; and Jem—with lighter heart and brighter face than he had had for many a day—sat down with Patience to their cheerful tea. No cloud of troubled feeling hung over Patience—the personal sacrifice that is made to God gives a present as well as a future reward; and Jem could scarcely believe the change for the better he saw in her. It seemed as if the Lady's piece of money—that gift of tenderness,—true to the feeling which bestowed it, was not only to possess a power to soothe through years of trial, but, when at last parted from, was to yield more present comfort and peace, even than when possessed; while the endless future alone can make manifest the results of what is so given, as this treasured possession of Patience—in love, and faith, and prayer! From that first Sabbath at Church, Patience improved daily in health. Their infant, little Peace by name, grew strong and merry when more with its mother in the open air. Patience could not at once recover her strength, yet the home of Jem again wore its cheerful aspect.

When May had given place to June, the preparations at the Hall were completed. All that was the work of the builder's art had been renewed, or fresh adorned; only one room had been left unentered by the repairer's step—it was the room that had been his sister's which Herbert had made his own, affection invested the faded adornments of that room with more attraction than any power of art could have imparted. Around the mansion, the stately trees and verdant slopes wore as fresh an aspect as when they first put on the emerald brightness of the spring. Tidings had arrived in the village, of the Squire having been married abroad: and now the day was fixed for his return, with his bride and mother, to the Hall.

The appointed day arrived, and the early stir of preparation was general. No gifts had been ordered by the Squire to celebrate the event; well he knew that his presence—his heart, and mind, his eye, and voice—would be a gift more prized than any, by villagers whose affections had grown around him from his boyhood. But orders were given by him for all the park-gates to be opened, that those who wished might receive him, on his return to reside among them, there, where he first had parted from them at his father's side. None were slow to go forth to the welcome—all dressed in festal garments, with the look of expectant gladness, they waited and watched. The tenantry had gone forward on horseback, a few miles; while William, steward of the farms, mounted on Black Beauty, stood at the grand entrance-gate. Four had been named as the hour; and now it struck from the great stable-clock. Then the scattered groups stood up from the greensward; and children took their parents' hands in questioning excitement. William rode on Black Beauty—who chafed at his long holding in—once down the broad walks of the Park, and shouted a request that all would stand off at the arrival, then back again quickly to his post at the great entrance-gate. Ringers had been stationed by William in the first village-church where the Squire had property, and as soon as the long line of tenantry returning and escorting the Squire were seen from that village-steeple, the bells were to strike up a peal. A watcher was set on the tower of the next village-church, and as soon as he heard the signal of approach, the solitary bell in that tower was to send on the tidings—over hill and valley, over the green waving corn and the yet unmown grass—to a watcher on the tower of their own village-church, then were their own bells to ring out the welcome heard from far. All hushed their breath to listen for the first distant sound—too impatient to wait for nearer tidings, trusting to catch from their friendly hills an echo to the first joyous peal. And who could wonder? Had not he, who now drew near, made their sorrows and joys their welfare and happiness, his own?—not by general dispensations of kindness, but by that frank and personal intercourse, which binds the heart with the tie of devoted affection—a tie far stronger, far higher and deeper, than that of mere personal gratitude for favours received. Had they not seen his warm feeling gush forth,—seen his active sympathy spring to the surface at the sight or hearing of trouble or sorrow of theirs? Was not the quick glance of his boyhood's eye, his generous utterance, familiar to many assembled there? Who would not come forth to receive in his manhood, the boy who had toiled in the ditch over old Willy's log,—who had climbed the thatcher's ladder to lay in an armful of straw, in the eager gladness of his heart at effacing the neglect of the poor man's oppressor! The whole village might have received gifts on some stately occasion, in some stately manner, by the boy provided with the means for the large bestowment; but it would not have bound the heart of the village to that boy like one free spontaneous effort—such as Herbert's had been, bearing witness to his self-forgetfulness in the poor man's distress. And was he not the brother of her who, to them, had seemed an angel upon Earth? Had he not followed in her gentle steps with his manly power—when once aroused to a sense of their blessedness; and had not the light of her life shone reflected on them? Then might the deep well-spring of feeling that had followed her to Heaven, break forth again to welcome his return to his home! True loyalty is happily a contagious emotion, and many a heart beat quicker, and many a cheek glowed with feeling that day, in those that did but estimate the event by the expectation of others.

The servants had now gathered to the door; the men, in their livery of dark blue and white, stood in two lines extending one on each side the steps; while the maids stood assembled in the entrance-hall. Again and again some eager listener said, "I heard the bells strike up—I am pretty sure I did!" But, no, it could not have been, for their own village tower stood still silent. At length William, the farm-steward, turned Black Beauty's head round, and facing the people and the servants, waved his hat above his head, then replacing it, turned instantly back again, standing sideways by the gate—he had caught the sound of the distant peal! Breathlessly the people now listened, and in a few minutes more their own village chime struck full on the ear, then the throng pressed side by side, as near as might be to the broad carriage sweep, while on pealed the bells; till the sound of many trampling hoofs was heard along the road. Still on they rang, till full in sight came the travelling-carriage, with its four horses and blue postilions; then the people raised a shout, and the tenantry who followed lifted their hats and joined the welcome cheers; through the great gate the carriage dashed, and William held his hat above his head, scarcely able to restrain Black Beauty's excited spirit; and his eye glanced up from his master's face, to where young Mercy sat behind—the village maiden back from the foreign land, pale with her own deep feeling, and the sound of that thrilling welcome. The carriage stopped at the Hall-door, and the tenantry dismounted and held their horses in hand. The Squire stepped from the carriage, and led his mother in to the care of her faithful servants; then returning handed out his Lady, and waving his hand to the people, led her within. William riding up, dismounted, and slipping Black Beauty's bridle over his arm, took down the orphan Mercy from the carriage with a brother's softened welcome—she wore mourning for the grandmother lost in her absence, who had filled the place of both parents to her, and her eyes were filled with the tears of mingled feelings. Then a servant brought a message to William from the Hall, and he instantly mounted Black Beauty again, and riding down the walks shouted, "The Squire begs you will be seated on the grass." Servants quickly appeared bearing between them trays of cake, and baskets filled with bottles of wine, all prepared by the Squire's orders in readiness beforehand. Then rising, the people breathed—not with a shout—but in a low murmur, a blessing on the head they had seen from its childhood uncovered beneath their roofs and among them; a blessing on the Squire's Lady; and a blessing on his mother. The Squire stood at the open window looking down upon them and hearing the thrice-repeated blessing; and his Lady at his side; and his heart filled with thankfulness that his tenants and dependants were his friends. Then the Squire turned away from the window, and the pe ›ple took their refreshment all seated on the grass, till the Squire came out, and his Lady on his arm; they stood on the first Hall-step, and the people rose in silence, and he said in a voice not loud but clear —a voice whose tones were all familiar, "God bless you, my friends, and enable us to retain your affection. We thank you for your welcome." And then he came down with his Lady; and he passed slowly among the people with his friendly greeting, and his Lady at his side—and all the time the village-bells rang out the same glad peal.

The eye of the Squire soon sought out Jem, well he knew his heart would be among the first to welcome him there, but he could nowhere discover his figure. At last he saw him, with his dog close behind him, his infant on his arm, and Patience at his side, at the further edge of the assembly, so he made his way up to him. The dog knew the Squire, and sprang forward to greet him, and leaped up licking his hand, and the Squire caressed him as he passed on to Jem, and said in his kind cheerful tone, "Well, Jem, do you pretend to be the last to welcome home your friend?" His beatiful Lady stood beside the Squire, and said with a smile, "I know the name of Jem! Is this your wife and child?" When Patience heard hei speak she looked up at her face, then falling on her knee, she caught hold of that Lady's dress and, pressing it to her lips, looked up again into her face, exclaiming, "O dearest Lady!"—It was the Lady Gertrude! And faint with long standing and overcome with feeling, poor Patience fell back upon the arm of Jem, who laid her gently on the grass, and knelt beside her. The Squire said, "Bring water! And fetch the gamekeeper's light cart to carry her home!" And Jem looked up and said, "She has been ill for months, and was but just getting over it, only I persuaded her to come with me to-day,—but it's been all over too much for her!" And the Lady Gertrude looked on the pale face of Patience—pale with her late long illness, but she saw no trace there of that early misery, that had left its impression so strongly in her heart—she did not know her to have been that child! Women had gathered round, Mrs. Smith and Rose were by this time with Patience, and the Squire and his Lady passed on; but as they returned towards the Hall, the Lady Gertrude said to the Squire, "They are still there, let us ask how Jem's wife is now;" so they stopped and the little close-gathered circle opened, and the Lady Gertrude said, "How is she now?" Patience was still seated on the grass, leaning on the arm of Jem, but she had revived, and now seeing their Lady again, she said, "O, Jem, she is not gone! ask if I may speak to her?" And the Lady Gertrude heard the words, and saw the flush suffuse the cheek of Patience, and kneeling on one knee upon the grass, beside her, she laid her hand upon the clasped hands of Patience, and said, "You are better now, you will soon recover this!" But Patience looking up said, "O, forgive me dearest Lady! I was that poor child you comforted! it was you that first put feeling into my froze-up heart! and I thought I should never have seen you again, and then to see you stand there—it wholly overcame me!" Tears came to that Lady's eyes, and she said, "Are you indeed the same? then I am come to live near you now, and and as I saw you in sorrow, so I hope I shall often see you in joy! You may be sure I shall soon come to your cottage!"

Jem had heard all about the love of Patience for that heavenly child that had come to her in her misery, and he looked upon that beautiful Lady kneeling there, with eyes of reverence and wonder; and tears were in the Squire's eyes as he stood there—but he did not speak a word; and Mrs. Smith and Rose with little Peace in her arms, and the women standing round—looked on astonished; but the light cart drove up, and the Squire returned with his Lady to the Hall, and Patience was taken back to her home, and so her heart's long desire was fulfilled—beyond all she had ever thought; and she quickly recovered strength, and the voice of joy and health was heard again in her dwelling.

Waggons and carts carried home the rejoicing people; and those near at hand returned on foot. And now the sun went down, and the long soft shadows fell over lawn and wood. Mrs. Clifford stood at the window with her children, and gazed on the slopes where the welcoming throng had been, and said, "It was too much for me to look upon, but not too much to feel the deepest thankfulness for!" and her son looked on her in answering tenderness. And then the Squire asked his Lady, if she missed the mountains from the landscape, that she had been used to from her childhood! And she replied, "O, human hearts are better than the hills, and stronger too in their encircling power! I know not where on Earth I could be so happy as here. And meeting, the first thing, with that poor child, whom I have thought of in her sorrow through so many years, seems to me a bright earnest of good." The sun went down, and the fervent feelings of that day reposed in the quiet of night's restful hours.

And now we must take leave of our ministering children,—who have all outgrown their childhood; —to write of and for childhood being all that we promised from the beginning. We have only to ask the children who read this story, whether they are also ministering children? This story has been written to show, as in a picture, what ministering children are. There is no child upon Earth, who may not be a ministering child: because the Holy Spirit of God, even the blessed Comforter Himself, will come to every one who aks for Him. Even the beloved Son of God, when He came down from Heaven to earth, came to minister to those who were in need—He Himself tells us so. And God sends His holy angels down to Earth to be ministering spirits here. The youngest child of God who is able to understand anything, can learn to be a ministering child! therefore, all who pray to God as their Heavenly Father, must try in every way they can to minister to others; and then one day they will go where there is no want, and no sorrow, and no sin, but only fullness of joy and pleasures for evermore—in their Heavenly Father's presence in glory; and there they will see those whom they comforted, and taught to know the love of God their Saviour upon Earth. "And so shall they be ever with the Lord;" "and God shall wipe away all tears from their eyes; and there shall be no more death, neither sorrow, nor crying, neither shall there be any more pain; for the former things will be passed away." Rev. xxi. 4.

END OF VOL. II.

www.ingramcontent.com/pod-product-compliance
Lightning Source LLC
LaVergne TN
LVHW010544110826
845149LV00003B/561

* 9 7 8 1 4 1 8 1 8 7 7 8 1 *